This is a continuation in the series of publications produced by the Center for Advanced Concepts and Technology (ACT), which was created as a "skunk works" with funding provided by the CCRP under the auspices of the Assistant Secretary of Defense (NII). This program has demonstrated the importance of having a research program focused on the national security implications of the Information Age. It develops the theoretical foundations to provide DoD with information superiority and highlights the importance of active outreach and dissemination initiatives designed to acquaint senior military personnel and civilians with these emerging issues. The CCRP Publication Series is a key element of this effort.

Check our Web site for the latest CCRP activities and publications.

www.dodccrp.org

DoD Command and Control Research Program

Assistant Secretary of Defense (NII)
&
Chief Information Officer

Dr. Linton Wells, II (Acting)

Principal Deputy Assistant Secretary of Defense (NII)

Dr. Linton Wells, II

Special Assistant to the ASD(NII)
&
Director, Research and Strategic Planning

Dr. David S. Alberts

Library of Congress Cataloging-in-Publication Data

Alberts, David S. (David Stephen), 1942-
Power to the Edge: Command and Control in the Information Age / David S. Alberts, Richard E. Hayes.
    p. cm.
 ISBN 1-893723-13-5
 1. Command and control systems--United States. 2. Information warfare--United States. 3. United States--Armed Forces--Reorganization. 4. Military art and science--Effect of technological innovations on--United States. I. Hayes, Richard E., 1942- II. Title.
 UB212.A43 2003
 355.3'3041--dc21

                                                        2003007597

1st printing June 2003
2nd printing June 2004
3rd printing April 2005

Information Age Transformation Series

Power
to the
Edge

Command...

Control...

in the

Information Age

David S. Alberts

Richard E. Hayes

with a Foreword by John Stenbit

CCRP
Publication
Series

Table of Contents

List of Figures

Acknowledgements

Working on this book has given us the opportunity to discuss important issues with a wide variety of talented professionals. The positive spirit with which our ideas were received, challenged, and debated has helped us to clarify our thoughts and their presentation. We owe a debt of gratitude to all those who have generously contributed their time to engage with us.

Many will recognize that the core idea behind this volume originated through interactions with the current Assistant Secretary of Defense for NII, Mr. John Stenbit. Equally valuable have been the interactions with his Principal Deputy, Dr. Linton Wells. In addition, Mr. John Garstka, currently in the Office of Force Transformation, has provided ongoing commentary and suggestions as these ideas were conceptualized and developed.

The Information Superiority Working Group (ISWG), a voluntary organization of senior professionals from government, industry, and academia that meets monthly in the Washington, D.C. area under the sponsorship of the DoD Command and Control Research Program (CCRP), was the first to hear and see many of these ideas. They debated them vigorously at every opportunity. Its core members include Michael Bell, Peter Brooks, Jim Hazlett, Paul Hiniker, John Garstka, Cliff Leiberman, Julia Loughran, Chris MacNulty, Mark Mandeles, Dan Oertel, Don Owen, Peter Perla, Dennis Popiela, John Porier, Mark Sinclair, Edward Smith, Stuart Starr, Eugene Visco, and Larry Wiener. This group was also generous in providing a rapid and thorough reading of the manuscript.

Broader input was also sought by sending the manuscript to members of a NATO working group even after its charter had expired. Those members who were able to respond in the short time available (Tim Bailey, Paul Chouinard, Cornelius d'Huy, Uwe Dompke, Dean Hartley, Reiner K. Huber, Don Kroening, Stef Kurstjens, Nicholas Lambert, Georges Lascar, Christian Manac'h, Graham Mathieson, Jim Moffat, Orhun Molyer, Valdur Pille, David Signori, Mark Sinclair, Mink Spaans, Stuart Starr, Swen Stoop, Hans Olav Sundfor, Klaus Titze, Andreas Tolk, Corinne Wallshein, and John Wilder) represent eight countries and have helped us to make certain that the ideas are clearly stated, represent more than just U.S. views, and are expressed in a way that will be "universally" understood.

Our international colleagues have also played an important role in developing many of these concepts. The idea of *agility* as a key concept first emerged in a U.S./UK workshop discussion and has been matured through interactions with Anthony Alston, Simon Atkinson, Wing Cmdr Q Dixon, Roland

Edwards, Richard Ellis, Julie Gadsen, Merfyn Lloyd, Graham Mathieson, Nigel Paling, and Jonathan Williams. Those interactions have been the basis for ongoing workshops that now involve research and development professionals from Australia, Sweden, Canada, and several other NATO countries. They were most recently assembled in December 2002 for a workshop on Conceptual Frameworks and Measurement of Network Centric Warfare. A number of the individuals at that workshop also reviewed the manuscript for us and provided rich and valuable insights.

Particularly valuable comments and ideas were provided by Ed Smith, Chris MacNulty, Richard Ivanetich, and Gina Kingston, whose detailed and thoughtful feedback demonstrated dedication to both the subject matter and the creation of a well written book.

Key members of the staff at Evidence Based Research also provided important feedback. Daniel Maxwell, David Noble, Dennis Leedom, David Signori, and Kimberly Holloman all provided substantive thoughts.

Mr. Joseph Lewis, Mr. Eric Cochrane, and Mr. Brian Davis cheerfully performed research, fact checking, and sourcing. Mr. Lewis proved his versatility by also creating the graphics for the volume (including the cover) and acting as primary editor for the text. He prepared the manuscript for the printer and managed the printing process.

David S. Alberts   Richard E. Hayes

Foreword
by John Stenbit

O ne can view the history of mankind as a
journey of empowerment, conspicuously
marked at critical junctures by the synergic combination of a particular technological advance
and an innovative social adaptation that
together eliminate a debilitating constraint. The
result is a leap to a new isoquant of productivity.
This book explores a leap now in progress, one
that will transform not only the U.S. military but
all human interactions and collaborative
endeavors. *Power to the edge* is a result of technological advances that will, in the coming decade,
eliminate the constraint of bandwidth, free us
from the need to know a lot in order to share a
lot, unfetter us from the requirement to be synchronous in time and space, and remove the last
remaining technical barriers to information
sharing and collaboration.

Our behaviors and the architectures and characteristics of our systems are driven by economics,
in this case the economics of information. The

dawn of the Information Age was ushered in by Moore's Law.[1] As the cost of computing fell, we stopped focusing our attentions on conserving available computing resources and began to be inefficient consumers of computing resources. Since bandwidth remained relatively scarce and costly, we distributed processing power widely but minimized the frequency and nature of information exchanges. Until quite recently, networking was too expensive for us to realize the value proposition embodied in Metcalfe's Law.[2] Advances in communications technologies gave rise to Gilder's Law[3] and provided an opportunity to be more robustly networked. As bandwidth becomes ever less costly and more widely available, we will be able to not only allow people to process information as they see fit but also allow multiple individuals and organizations to have direct and simultaneous access to information and to each other. We will also be able to support richer interactions between and among individuals.

This has profound implications for the way that information can be disseminated, moving us from a *smart smart push* approach to a *smart pull* approach. We began the Information Age by pushing information to those deemed to have a need for it. Of course, the owners of the information needed to be smart both with respect to knowing what information was important to whom, and in a circuit-based communications infrastructure, they also needed to be smart about how to reach them. Hence, *smart smart push*. In addition, they needed to be synchronous in time and space. This approach to information sharing saved on the scarce resources of its age: processing, storage, and bandwidth.

The move to broadcast (*smart push*) removed one of the "smarts," the requirement for the sender to know everyone who needed the information and allowed (with mobile listening devices) the receiver to be asynchronous in space. It did not remove the need to know what information was of interest nor the constraint that the parties needed to be synchronous in time. Broadcast saves bandwidth but wastes processing and storage, capabilities that were becoming increasing less expensive.

The advent of e-mail removed the need to be synchronous in both time and space but did not remove the requirement for the sender to know what was of interest and how to address those with the need for the information. Finally, the advent of networking and browser technology enabled a move to *smart pull*, freeing us from the constraints to be synchronous in time and space and eliminating the need for owners of information to know what is important to whom and how to get in touch with them. It enables the widespread information sharing that is a prerequisite for shared awareness and the Information Age approach to command and control described in this book.

The opportunities created by these breakthroughs are beginning to be pursued by innovators in DoD and elsewhere who are exploring new ways of accomplishing the tasks at hand. In the final analysis, the success of these transformational efforts will be directly related to our ability to bring information to bear in our warfighting and other national security missions, as well as in the business processes necessary to acquire capabilities and support operations.

The entry fee is a ubiquitous, secure, robust, trusted, protected, and routinely used wide-bandwidth net that is populated with the information and information services that our forces need. With *power to the edge* as our mantra, we see the solders, sailors, marines, airmen, and civilians of DoD all connected by a network that they can trust and that can facilitate the building of trusted relationships. Empowered by access to quality information and unconstrained by artificial boundaries and stovepipes, there is no limit to what the men and women of DoD can accomplish.

My organization is dedicated to building the Global Information Grid that, in the near future, will have put in place the policies, technologies, processes, and systems to enable people to have the accesses they need to information and each other. While we devote ourselves tirelessly to this mission, others will need to explore innovative ways to leverage the opportunities created by these information capabilities. This book will, hopefully, raise the level of awareness that it is time for new command and control concepts, and even inspire some to jump in and explore the possibilities.

Our future success requires that we think about information and relationships differently. We need to move from a set of monopoly suppliers of information to an information marketplace. Only by doing this will we be able to ensure that our forces will have the variety of views and perspectives necessary to make sense out of the complex situations that they will face. And only by moving to marketplaces can we ensure that our information collection and analysis capabilities will dynamically evolve to changing circumstances. Similarly, we need to move rapidly from a push-oriented dissemination process to a pull-oriented one. This is the only way to satisfy the needs of a heterogeneous population of information users.

Our approach to interoperability needs to change as well. Given the rate of advancing technology, we need to move from an approach based upon application standards to one based upon data standards. We need to give users of information the opportunity to use the applications that make sense to them while maintaining the ability to exchange information. Finally, we need to pay a great deal more attention to supporting peer-to-peer relationships and information exchanges that transcend individual systems and organizations. Doing these things will empower the edge of the organization and enable us to change the way we approach everything we do.

Indeed, *power to the edge* is the principle that we have chosen to guide us as we rethink our policies, organizations, and processes. This book does not profess to have the answers, but it makes some provocative observations, raises the right questions, and suggests a way ahead. I hope you'll feel glad that you took the time to read it.

NOTES

1   Moore's Law - The observation that the logic density of silicon integrated circuits has closely followed the curve (bits per square inch) = $2^{\wedge}(t - 1962)$ where t is time in years; that is, the amount of information storable on a given amount of silicon has roughly doubled every year since the technology was invented. This relation, first uttered in 1964 by semiconductor engineer Gordon Moore (who co-founded Intel 4 years later), held until the late 1970s, at which point the doubling period slowed to 18 months.

2   Metcalfe's Law states that the value of a network is proportional to the square of the number of nodes in the network. METCALFE'S LAW AND LEGACY, was first published in Forbes ASAP, September 13, 1993.

3   Gilder's Law, proposed in 1997, states that the total bandwidth of communication systems triples every 12 months.

Preface

*P*ower to the Edge is the latest book in the Information Age Transformation Series, and in a sense it completes the articulation of a vision of DoD Transformation and an approach to achieving it. With the publication of this book, readers have a reference "library" consisting of not only the books in this series, but also the previous CCRP funded and published books to draw upon.

Basic information about the nature of the Information Age and its implications for national security and the military can be found in the three-volume *Information Age Anthology*. The classic volume *Network Centric Warfare*, republished by many public and private organizations in several languages, provides the earliest detailed articulation of the set of tenets that link a robustly networked force to dramatically increased combat power. It describes how information coupled with changes in C2 can transform military organizations.

Understanding Information Age Warfare updates and expands upon NCW by introducing collaboration and the cognitive domains into the discussion. It also provides a common language for articulating the issues and builds the foundation for the development of a detailed NCW Conceptual Framework. It also begins the task of specifying measures that can be used to provide guideposts for the journey of transformation.

Information Age Transformation focuses its attention on the nature and process of transformation, identifying critical path items including the need for creating conditions for disruptive innovation and a variety of experimentation activities.

Two other volumes deal with issues essential to transformation. *The Code of Best Practice for Experimentation* distills a wealth of practical experience and provides a guide for those involved in these activities. *Effects Based Operations* completes the NCW value chain, explaining the link from network-centric organizations and processes to mission outcomes. It provides the link between the why and how of an operation.

Power to the Edge was written at the request of John Stenbit, the ASD(NII) who wanted to develop a broader understanding of the principles being used to develop policy, make decisions regarding investments in C4ISR, and provide oversight of ongoing DoD programs and related activities that will provide the ubiquitous, secure, wideband network that people will trust and use, populate with high quality information, and use for developing shared awareness, collaborating effectively, and synchronizing their actions.

As with each of our books, our aim was to provide our readers with material that would increase awareness of emerging ideas and approaches and stimulate discussion. We do not pretend to have all of the answers, but we do feel that the ideas expressed here are worthy of your attention.

David S. Alberts

Director, Research and Strategic Planning (NII)

Washington, DC

2003

Chapter 1

Introduction

The events of September 11, 2001, signaled an inflection point between the remnants of the security environment dominated by the symmetrical calculus of the Cold War and the uncertainties and asymmetries of the 21st century security environment. The risks and challenges of an uncertain security landscape are exacerbated by the exponential decrease in the size and cost of weapons of mass destruction and disruption, their proliferation, and the ever more richly connected and interdependent world of the 21st century.

At the same time, the complexity of military operations is increasing as strategic, operational, and tactical levels merge, as operations serve a mixture of military and civil objectives, and as operations are carried out by coalitions of the willing. Increasingly, military commanders are faced with the conundrum of reconciling traditional military operations with overall mission and national policy objectives. The link between military effectiveness and policy effectiveness can no longer be assumed. Effects-Based Operations (EBO)[1] change the dimensionality of effectiveness and explicitly connect effects in the military arena to effects in the other arenas.

While it is hard for some to believe, we are arguably in a more dangerous world with less means to defend our vital interests, with institutions that are less well structured and practiced to carry out needed operations. This is because the emerging threats are different and are continuing to evolve, as well as because our legacy force structure and concepts of operation are not well suited for the tasks at hand, nor are they agile enough to keep abreast of the continuing changes. Agility will prove to be the most important single characteristic of military forces in the 21st century. *The road to agility is paved with information.* This volume focuses on how Information Age technology will allow basic changes in how military forces are organized, trained, and employed to generate the agility needed to defeat (some might say *prevent* or *dissolve*) asymmetric threats. One of the most visible military historians, Martin van Creveld, has gone so far as to argue that the security environment is changing so radically that militaries as we know them will soon become obsolete and be replaced by qualitatively different organizations.[2]

LEVERAGING THE POWER OF INFORMATION

This sea change in the security environment comes at a time when the Information Age is changing the calculus of wealth and power. The Information Age is transforming information from an ordinary commodity into a "golden goose" that can replicate and multiply both information and its value at little or no cost. The Information Age is also exponentially reducing the costs of communication, promising to make the dream of virtually unlimited bandwidth a reality in the coming decade.

The emergence of the Information Age offers us the opportunity to leverage new sources of power to meet the challenges we face. That is exactly what the transformation of the Department of Defense (DoD) is all about. DoD transformation seeks to reorient us and focus our attention on emerging and future missions, change the way we fight (operate) to leverage Information Age concepts and technologies, and change our business processes to make us an Information Age organization. Transformation is about continuous adaptation to the Information Age. A recent report to Congress on Network Centric Warfare began its executive summary by saying that "Network Centric Warfare is no less than the embodiment of an Information Age transformation of the DoD."[3]

This report, coming as it did less than 3 years after the publication of *Network Centric Warfare*,[4] a book that provided the first comprehensive treatment of how militaries could create and leverage the power of information, is testimony to the pace of change we are experiencing. In the interim, several more books[5] and countless articles[6] have been devoted to exploring this topic. Funds have been shifted to enhance DoD infostructure to provide the "net," populate it with information, and protect it.[7] More attention has been paid to interoperability. The battlefields of Bosnia, Kosovo, Afghanistan, and Iraq have provided additional proofs of concept of the value of network-centric capabilities.[8] Joint and Service experiments[9] have focused explicitly and implicitly on exploring the tenets of Network Centric Warfare and/or

Operations (NCW/NCO). However, despite this increasing activity and undeniable progress toward network-centricity, many still miss the most profound implications that NCW/NCO has for military organizations.

The path to NCO is forked. One road, often called "modernization," is the straightest and most clearly signed. Traveling this road is clearly within the comfort zone of the institution (DoD) and most of its members. Unfortunately, this road will lead us only to incremental improvements and, ultimately, to a dead end. The improvements attained, however impressive, will fall short, not only of the potential of network-centricity, but more importantly, they will not enable us to meet the mission challenges of the 21st century. This is the road that many seem to have embarked upon, despite a high-level commitment to transformation. The other, less traveled road (actually it may appear more as a path) leads to a *disruptive* transformation of command and control (C2) that is central to all military organizations and processes, the first since the early to mid-19th century.[10] This transformation must focus on C2, where information is translated into actionable knowledge. Without a transformation of C2, it is far less likely that we will be able to meet the challenges that lie ahead. A transformation of C2 provides us with the best opportunity to achieve the one organizational characteristic that is sure to stand us in good stead for the foreseeable future–*agility.*

POWER TO THE EDGE

The purpose of this book is to explain why we must go down the road less traveled, why current command and control concepts, organizations, and systems are not up to the task at hand, and present the approach to command and control and

C2 support systems that is needed. This approach is called *power to the edge.*

Power to the edge is about changing the way individuals, organizations, and systems relate to one another and work. *Power to the edge* involves the empowerment of individuals at the edge of an organization (where the organization interacts with its operating environment to have an impact or effect on that environment) or, in the case of systems, edge devices. Empowerment involves expanding access to information and the elimination of unnecessary constraints. For example, empowerment involves providing access to available information and expertise and the elimination of procedural constraints previously needed to deconflict elements of the force in the absence of quality information.

Moving power to the edge implies adoption of an *edge organization*, with greatly enhanced peer-to-peer interactions. Edge organizations also move senior personnel into roles that place them at the edge. They often reduce the need for middle managers whose role is to manage constraints and control measures. Command and control become unbundled. Commanders become responsible for creating initial conditions that make success more likely and exercise control by:

- Creating congruent command intent across the enterprise;

- Allocating resources dynamically; and

- Establishing rules of engagement and other control mechanisms that the fighting forces implement themselves.

Power to the edge, when fully achieved in each of the domains of warfare,[11] provides the conditions that allow NCW to reach its fully mature form–a self-synchronizing capability.

Efficient self-organization has been possible in the past (for example, see the discussion of the Battle of Trafalgar) when the key conditions were obtained (shared situation awareness, congruent command intent, professional competence, and trust). However, the information available and the need to interact effectively make it very difficult to achieve shared awareness and congruent command intent.

The ability of a force to conduct network-centric operations and to self-synchronize is closely related both to mission effectiveness and to force agility. Force agility includes *robustness*, the ability to maintain effectiveness over a range of conditions and circumstances. Thus, when *power to the edge* is fully realized, the very nature of an organization will have been transformed, as well as that organization's capabilities.

The adoption of *power to the edge* as a major organizing and operating principle for DoD is absolutely necessary if we are to maintain our military superiority in the 21st century. We are being driven to this, at a time when the U.S. military is considered by many to be "at the top of its game," by changes in the nature of the security challenges we face and the environment in which we need to operate. *Power to the edge* is the correct response to the increased uncertainty, volatility, and complexity associated with military operations. This is not a problem that is unique to the military domain,[12] but it is an integral part of the transition from the Industrial Age to the Information Age. The principles that we call *power to the edge* are inherent, but not fully explained, in the tenets of Network Centric Warfare. They are just beginning to be articulated elsewhere[13] as they represent an emerging understanding of how to survive in the Information Age, which has witnessed the breakdown of Industrial Age approaches and solutions to organization and management.

ORGANIZATION OF THE BOOK

This book begins with a discussion of the nature of command and control. It includes a distillation of the essence of command and control, providing definitions and identifying the enduring functions that must be performed in any military operation. Since there is no single approach to command and control that has yet to prove suitable for all purposes and situations, militaries throughout history have, to varying degrees, employed a variety of approaches to commanding and controlling their forces. A representative sample of the most successful of these approaches is reviewed and their implications are discussed.

Following this discussion of command and control is a look at the nature of Industrial Age militaries, their inherent properties, and their inability to develop the level of interoperability and agility needed in the Information Age. The Industrial Age has had a profound effect on the nature and the conduct of warfare and on military organizations. As the immediate predecessor of the Information Age, Industrial Age command and control represents our current point of departure and serves as a baseline that can be used in identifying and understanding the nature of the changes required. A discussion of the characteristics of Industrial Age militaries and command and control is used to set the stage for an examination of their suitability for Information Age missions and environments. The Industrial Age military's competitive posture is then assessed in terms of its ability (or inability) to deal with the complexities, uncertainties, risks, and dynamics of the 21st century security environment.

The nature of the changes associated with Information Age technologies and the desired characteristics of Information Age militaries, particularly the command and control capabilities needed to meet the full spectrum of mission challenges, are introduced and discussed in detail. Two interrelated force characteristics that transcend any mission or set of missions are of particular importance in the Information Age—interoperability and agility. Each of these key topics is treated in a separate chapter.

Command and control, as it has been understood for most of the 20th century, has evolved from a set of assumptions about *fog* and *friction* in warfare. Information Age technologies have dramatically changed the economics of information, which in turn has given rise to new forms of organization and approaches to command and control. The basic concepts (*power* and *the edge*) necessary to understand *power to the edge* are introduced so that the reader can view the discussion of traditional military organizations and approaches to command and control from an Information Age perspective. The discussion of *power to the edge* continues. The advantages of moving power from the center to the edge and achieving control indirectly, rather than directly, are discussed as they apply to both military organizations and the architectures and processes of the C4ISR systems that support them.

Adopting *power to the edge* principles and practices not only has implications for the nature and capabilities of the infostructure required and the way information is employed by an organization, but it also has implications for each of the other components of a mission capability package (MCP),[14] and for the business side of DoD. These are briefly discussed. The book concludes with a set of observations about where we are and what needs to be done to enable us to make this new command and control approach work for us.

NOTES

1   Smith, Edward. *Effects Based Operations: Applying Network Centric Warfare in Peace, Crisis, and War.* Washington, DC: CCRP Publication Series. 2003.
    Hayes, Richard E., and Sue Iwanski. "Analyzing Effects Based Operations (EBO) Workshop Summary." *PHALANX.* Vol 35, No 1. Alexandria, VA: Military Operations Research Society. March 2002.

2   Creveld, Martin van. *The Transformation of War.* New York, NY: The Free Press. 1991.

3   *Network Centric Warfare Department of Defense Report to Congress.* Washington, DC. July 2001.

4   Alberts, David S., John J. Garstka, and Frederick P. Stein. *Network Centric Warfare: Developing and Leveraging Information Superiority.* 2nd Edition (Revised). Washington, DC: CCRP Publication Series. 1999.

5   Herman, Mark. *Measuring the Effects of Network-Centric Warfare.* Vol 1. Technical report prepared for the Director of Net Assessment, Office of the Secretary of Defense. McLean, VA: Booz Allen & Hamilton. April 28, 1999.
    Alberts, David S. *Information Age Transformation: Getting to a 21st Century Military.* Washington, DC: CCRP Publication Series. 2002.
    Alberts, David S., John Garstka, Richard E. Hayes, and David T. Signori. *Understanding Information Age Warfare.* Washington, DC: CCRP Publication Series. 2001.

6   For example: Garstka, John J. "Network Centric Warfare: An Overview of Emerging Theory." *PHALANX.* Alexandria, VA: MORS. December 2000.
    Cebrowski, VADM Arthur K. and John J. Garstka. "Network-Centric Warfare: Its Origin and Future." *Proceedings.* Volume 124/1/1,139. Annapolis, MD: U.S. Naval Institute. January 1998. pp. 28-35.
    Stein, Fred. "Observations on the Emergence of Network Centric Warfare." Proceedings for the 1998 Command and Control Research and Technology Symposium. Washington, DC: CCRP Publication Series. June 1998.
    Leopold, George. "Networks: DoD's First Line of Defense." *Tech Web.* October 1997.

http://www.techweb.com/wire/news/1997/10/1013dod.html. (Apr 1, 2003)

Brewin, Bob. "DoD Lays Groundwork for Network-Centric Warfare." *Federal Computer Week*. November 1997. http://www.fcw.com/fcw/articles/1997/FCW_110197_1171.asp. (Apr 1, 2003)

7   ASD(NII) CIO Homepage. Office of the Secretary of Defense. http://www.c3i.osd.mil/homepage.html#goals. (Apr 1, 2003)
Goal #1 - Make information available on a network that people depend on and trust.
Goal #2 - Populate the network with new, dynamic sources of information to defeat the enemy.
Goal #3 - Deny the enemy comparable advantages and exploit weaknesses.

8   Wentz, Larry, ed. *Lessons from Bosnia: The IFOR Experience*. Washington, DC: CCRP Publication Series. April 1998.
Wentz, Larry, ed. *Lessons from Kosovo: The KFOR Experience*. Washington, DC: CCRP Publication Series. July 2002.
Verton, Dan. "IT at the Heart of Shock and Awe: With U.S. Invasion, Era of Network-Centric Warfare has Dawned." *Computerworld*. Mar 13, 2003. http://www.computerworld.com/hardwaretopics/hardware/story/0,10801,79853,00.html. (Apr 1, 2003)
Salkever, Alex. "The Network is the Battlefield" *Computerworld Online*. Jan 7, 2003. http://www.businessweek.com/technology/content/jan2003/tc2003017_2464.htm. (Apr 1, 2003)

9   Unified Vision 01:
http://www.jfcom.mil/about/experiments/uv01.htm (Feb 1, 2003)
Millennium Challenge 02:
http://www.jfcom.mil/about/experiments/mc02.htm (Feb 1, 2003)
Joint Expeditionary Forces Exercise:
http://afeo.langley.af.mil/gateway/jefx00.asp (Feb 1, 2003)
The Joint Mission Force: Transformation in the U.S. Pacific Command.
USCINCPAC J3. White Paper V.1.0 (DRAFT) February 2001.

10   Some would argue that conversion from foot and animal power to engine power created a major revolution by enhancing the mobility of platforms during the late 19th and 20th centuries.

11   Alberts, *Understanding*. pp. 10-14.

12   Alberts, David, and Daniel Papp. *Information Age Anthology, Volume I: The Nature of the Information Age*. Washington, DC: CCRP Publications. 2001.

13 Robertson, Bruce, and Valentin Sribar. *The Adaptive Enterprise: IT Infrastructure Strategies to Manage Change and Enable Growth*. Santa Clara, CA: Intel Press. 2001.

14 Alberts, David S. "Mission Capability Packages." Washington, DC: National Defense University Strategic Forum. Jan 14, 1995. Alberts, *Information Age Transformation*.

Chapter 2

Command and Control

Command and Control (C2) is the common military term for management of personnel and resources.[1] C2 is a relatively recent[2] term that for millennia was referred to as simply *command*. Command concepts both predate and have evolved separately from politics and industrial management. This is because warfare is qualitatively different from the management of other human enterprises by virtue of its time criticality and the high cost of error. Both of these characteristics of warfare and a preoccupation with *fog and friction*[3] have shaped thinking about C2.

DEFINITION OF COMMAND AND CONTROL

The official U.S. definition of the terms *C2* and *command* can be found in a Joint Chiefs of Staff Publication.[4] Command, as defined in JCS Pub. 1, includes "responsibility for effectively using available resources, planning the employment of, organizing, directing, coordinating, and controlling military forces for the accomplishment of assigned missions. It also includes the responsibility for health, welfare, morale, and discipline of assigned personnel." This definition subsumes control as a part of command. Many have tried to draw a distinction between command and control.[5] Distinctions that have been drawn include one between art (command) and science (control) and one between the commander (command) and staff (control). Much of the discussion is focused on a single commander, the one in charge. In fact, command and control in modern warfare is a distributed responsibility. Discussions of command and control are all too often sidetracked by inappropriate defenses of tradition, hero worship, and a misunderstanding of the enduring nature of command and control. The words are frequently used inconsistently despite the fact that they are enshrined in military jargon. It is one thing for Network Centric Warfare or Transformation to be misused and misinterpreted, since these terms are in their infancy, but the term *command* has been around for thousands of years and C2 has been around for more than half a century, with origins in the early part of the Industrial Age.

DOMAINS OF COMMAND AND CONTROL

Given that the term *command and control* encompasses as much as it does, its elements span all of the four domains of warfare (physical, information, cognitive, and social). C2 sensors, systems, platforms, and facilities exist in the physical domain.

The information collected, posted, pulled, displayed, processed, and stored exists in the information domain. The perceptions and understanding of what this information states and means exist in the cognitive domain. Also in the cognitive domain are the mental models, preconceptions, biases, and values that serve to influence how information is interpreted and understood, as well as the nature of the responses that may be considered. C2 processes and the interactions between and among individuals and entities that fundamentally define organization and doctrine exist in the social domain.

The principles of *power to the edge* can be applied to both the organization and management of work and the design and architecture of systems. Its application to the organization and management of work is primarily about C2 in the cognitive and social domains, while its application to the infostructure relates primarily to C2 in the physical and information domains.

ENDURING PRINCIPLES

Enabling a collection of individuals to accomplish a mission that requires their collective skills and energies requires command and control. It does not require a single commander nor does it require one or more individuals acting as controllers. Command and control are functions that need to be accomplished; however, they can be accomplished in a variety of different ways. Thus, the "enduring principles" of command and control are about the necessary and sufficient conditions for success in military operations, not how these were or are accomplished. At one point in time, it was the commander's responsibility to develop situation awareness and communicate the aspect(s) that subordinates needed in order to be effective. Situation awareness will always need to be developed and shared, but whose task this is and how it is accomplished are evolving.

Getting the job done involves things that need to be accomplished prior to undertaking a given task or mission and things that need to be done to accomplish the mission. Readiness is a function that needs to be accomplished prior to the undertaking of a mission. First, there must be an organization in place that has the characteristics required to accomplish a range of anticipated tasks. This includes policies, processes, and procedures. Second, individuals must be motivated, educated, trained, and practiced. Third, provisions need to be made for the collection of information, the sharing of information, and for interactions among individuals and organizations. Fourth, appropriate tools and equipment must be available. Also prior to undertaking a task, the need for and nature of the task must be articulated. This takes the form of command intent. Given the variety of elements involved in Information Age warfare and its effects-based orientation, command intent must be congruent across several elements (joint forces), coalition elements (combined), interagency partners, international organizations, and nongovernmental organizations.[6]

During the undertaking of the mission, those involved need to make sense of the situation and orchestrate the means to respond in a timely manner. These functions are performed iteratively with the means being adjusted dynamically in response to changes in the situation and/or command intent. Making sense of the situation is inherently dynamic. This implies that the functions associated with battlespace monitoring and the development of awareness are continuous processes.[7] Likewise, battlespace management, the adjustments of means, is also a continuous process.

Responsibility, authority, and accountability are essential features of command and control. C2 and organizational concepts and approaches that fail to distribute responsibility in an effective manner, fail to match responsibilities and authorities, or fail to properly hold individuals and organizations accountable for their actions (or inactions) will exhibit dysfunctional behaviors and have their effectiveness degraded. Errors of this type result in role gaps and role overlaps with serious consequences for military operations. There is a substantial literature that discusses responsibility, authority, and accountability as a function of organization and culture and documents the consequences of failures to properly balance the considerations involved.[8]

To summarize, the enduring principles of command and control are not about who accomplishes what tasks, nor how to accomplish them, but the *nature* of these tasks themselves. Traditions are often about responsibilities for how tasks are distributed (roles) and about how tasks are performed. They should not be presumed to be enduring.

Not surprisingly, voices are calling increasingly for a fundamental revisiting of the concepts of command and control free from the encumbrances of historical metaphors and paradigms. A growing number of those who are looking at command and control in the Information Age have concluded that the terms need to be clarified and brought into the 21st century.

Pigeau and McCann[9] recently offered their reconceptualization of command and control, defining them separately while maintaining a dependency between the terms. Interestingly, they start with a definition of control that goes beyond a simple engineering view of feedback to include personnel, facilities, and procedures, which in turn imply structures and processes. They observe that "control comes at a price" because it restricts flexibility. They offer the following formal definitions of control and command:

- "Control: those structures and processes devised by command to enable it and to manage risk."

- "Command: the creative expression of human will necessary to accomplish the mission."

Hence, they define control as the instrument of command. Command, as they define it, can be exercised by everyone in the enterprise. Pigeau and McCann explicitly highlight this implication and recognize its significance.[10] Using different words, they are making the case for moving from a concept of command that is tied to an individual commander to a concept of command that is widely distributed. This idea of distributed command was introduced in *Command Arrangements for Peace Operations* in recognition of (1) the absence of a single chain of command and (2) the variety of the players involved in peace operations. This idea was generalized beyond peace operations and appeared in the literature with the shift from "commander's" intent in *Network Centric Warfare* (1999) to "command" intent in *Understanding Information Age Warfare* (2001).[11]

SPECTRUM OF C2 APPROACHES

One of the most important findings from earlier research is that there was not, during the Industrial Age, a single "best" approach to (or philosophy of) command and control. We have twice published summaries of that literature[12] that describe half a dozen different philosophies that were used successfully in the 20th century by different military establishments. These were organized in terms of the degree of centralization involved, particularly at the theater or operational level of command. The key finding from reviewing the evidence from that era is that the correct C2 approach depends on several factors, including the:

- Warfighting environment–from static (trench warfare) to mobile (maneuver warfare);

- Continuity of communications across echelon (from cyclic to continuous);

- Volume and quality of information moving across echelon and function;

- Professional competence of the decisionmakers (senior officers at all levels of command) and their forces; and

- Degree of creativity and initiative the decisionmakers in the force, particularly the subordinate commanders, can be expected to exercise.

Six different philosophies were found in successful military organizations during the 20th century. When organized from most to least centralized, they imply a degree of central control based on the directives that are issued from the operational level of command. For the most centralized systems, these directives are detailed orders: what to do, when to do it, where to do it, and how to do it. Somewhat less centralized systems are termed *objective specific* because their operational level commands organize their directives around military objectives to be achieved, leaving the details of when, where, and how to the units. The least centralized command and control approaches can be identified by the fact that their operational level headquarters issue *mission specific* directives, which assign missions to forces, but leave decisions about how they are to be achieved up to subordinates. More specifically, the six different approaches are identified (from most to least centralized) as:

1. Cyclic

2. Interventionist

3. Problem-Solving

4. Problem-Bounding

5. Selective Control

6. Control Free

Cyclic

Cyclic C2 approaches are detailed orders issued on the basis of a regular schedule from the central command. This usually occurs when communications bandwidth is severely limited in comparison with the amount of information that must be exchanged, the actions of the operating units are interdependent and must be coordinated in detail, and the subordinate commanders and their forces lack the ability to exercise independent creativity (which may be because they lack adequate information or the degree of professional expertise required), so they must be expected to follow the plan with great energy to overcome its lack of flexibility. Cyclic C2 systems are best suited for static warfare situations where there is time to gather all the information at the center, make it available to senior commanders, have them make optimum decisions, and issue detailed directives and plans to the forces.

Cyclic C2 was adopted by the Soviets during World War II because they lacked the communications systems needed for richer exchanges, because Stalin demanded the ability to make all important decisions, because they were resource constrained and felt they needed a central control that would optimize their allocations, and because their commanders and forces lacked the professional skills to exercise creativity.[13] However, the USAF Air Tasking Order, developed during the 20th century, is also cyclic, based on a 72-hour cycle and controlling aircraft "by tail number" from theater level command centers. The rationale behind it is primarily the need for detailed coordination among the elements of the force and the intricate nature of air combat–linking surveillance, preparing the battlespace, assessing air defenses, defending our own forces, providing escorts and electronic warfare support, conducting strike operations, refueling in mid-air, coordinating fixed wing and rotary wing aircraft, conducting search and rescue operations, and assessing battle damage. In recent years, these ATOs have become somewhat more flexible by increasing the potential to create "on-call" missions and divert aircraft en route to exploit targets of opportunity. However, an ATO still functions (at this writing) on a 72-hour cycle.

Interventionist

Like cyclic C2, the interventionist model issues specific orders from the theater level. However, they have a greater communications capacity that allows them to intervene and change their directives at irregular intervals, particularly if an opportunity or threat emerges. The Cold War-era Soviet military was able to adopt this approach as the competence of their forces and the strength of their communications systems improved over time.[14]

Note, however, that the central command was still issuing orders to the operational units. To do this, the Soviets relied on "football plays." That is, they worked out a set of types of operations and the best ways to conduct them. For example, they had an ideal approach for a "breakthrough" operation, another one for a pincer movement, still another for defense of a river obstacle, and so forth. These were, in essence, optimized ways to accomplish military missions given the force structure of the USSR. These "plays" were learned in Soviet military schools, reviewed in detail in the war games, and practiced during their exercises. Like an American football team, each element of the force knew their role in each play and had practiced executing it over and over again. While this approach lacked potential for innovation and flexibility, it provided commanders with predictability as well as ways of controlling forces and measuring progress. For example, the artillery organizations knew where they should position themselves for each type of operation; the logistics trains understood their task in each type, and so forth. In some sense, the "modern" ATO approaches an interventionist philosophy.

Problem-Solving

The more centralized of the two C2 approaches in which the operational level headquarters concentrates on specifying the objectives for the elements of the force has been termed *problem-solving*. This approach does allow for innovation and flexibility by subordinate commanders, but does so within a set of constraints imposed by senior commanders. When this approach is used (and it has been common in the U.S. Army and Navy), the objectives are stated clearly and are accompanied by a set of milestones that stress what is to be accomplished and when (either against a time schedule or in terms of a sequence). Higher headquarters also constrain the assets (force elements, lift assets, etc.) available to accomplish these missions. They also typically include specific guidance about boundaries (who has the use of which roads, who is responsible for which areas) that helps to define the objectives and constrain subordinate choices. In essence, this approach is a challenge to the subordinates to solve the problem of accomplishing their missions within the constraints established by the senior commanders. It also explains why successful U.S. commanders during World War II were found to spend considerable time visiting with and hosting their superior commanders.[15] They were actively working to shape their future missions, acquire assets, establish beneficial boundaries, and reduce constraints.

Problem-Bounding

Research on NATO Cold War command and control revealed that the orders issued by U.K. officers to their forces were about one-third the length of those issued by U.S. NATO commanders in equivalent commands. Careful review of these documents showed that both were built around objectives. However, the U.K. officers provided many fewer milestones and constraints to their subordinates. They typically defined the objective(s) to be achieved, provided the assets (forces) to be employed, and minimal information about schedules and boundaries. They were rich in the number of contingencies identified, but relatively thin in detail about them. In other words, the mission(s) were offered to subordinates as problems, but much less detail was offered about how they would be solved. This approach was termed *problem-bounding*.

Research into World War II plans and operations has suggested the hypothesis that U.S. military organizations moved (over time and as they gained operational experience) from problem-solving to problem-bounding C2.[16] That is, as the competence and experience of all echelons of command increased, the degree of detail in the written plans decreased. In other words, more was left to the force elements. Professor Wayne Hughes, in his excellent book *Fleet Tactics*, points out that U.S. destroyer tactics in the Pacific evolved from very simple to much more complex arrangements as the ship commanders and their crews gained experience against the Japanese.[17] This would be consistent with the general theory underlying the spectrum of C2 approaches. However, U.S. doctrine and training did not change, probably because major operations continued to involve new forces (units that had just completed training) and commanders.

Selective Control

When the focus of directives moves up to missions, even more responsibility is placed on the subordinates in a C2 system. The modern Israeli system is the best example of a selective control approach, where the theater level headquarters is generally content to establish the initial conditions for success (providing very capable forces and assigning them general missions) and monitoring the situation to ensure no major threats or opportunities go undetected. This approach requires considerable capacity in the subordinate forces and trust in them by the higher headquarters. It also requires excellent information and awareness within the operating units. In essence, the approach relies on a series of "local optimums" as the elements of the force win engagements and battles that build toward the achievement of the overall mission.

However, a selective control philosophy still assumes that circumstances may arise in which the theater level will have to assert itself aggressively. Hence, it assumes considerable discipline on the part of the senior commanders in that they must work primarily to support and make subordinates effective, only intervening when major developments take the situation outside the set that their forces can deal with successfully. It also assumes that the subordinates will, if and when the theater commander decides to intervene, show the discipline needed to respond promptly and effectively to the new command intent.

Control Free

In the control-free approach, the primary role of the theater commander is to support the force—creating initial conditions that maximize the likelihood of mission accomplishment and providing the information and resources necessary for the force elements to succeed—including the new information and assets they require as the situation changes. The least centralized of the effective C2 philosophies identified from the Industrial Age experience is control-free—virtual autonomy for the subordinate force commander. This was the philosophy adopted by the German Army during World War II. A German Corps commander from this era had enormous discretion and decision authority, particularly early in the war before

Hitler began to micromanage the force and while it was led by highly professional officers. The philosophy was still largely intact even near the end of the war (despite the fact that the practice was very different in those theaters that attracted Hitler's attention). For example, when the Anzio landing took place, an experienced Corps commander who was in Italy with his staff to rest and recover was ordered to take command of all German forces in the area and contain the landing. He did so successfully.

Individual commanders with considerable confidence in their subordinates have been documented as using the control-free approach. For example, General Douglas MacArthur, when organizing his campaign to island hop and retake the Philippines, is reported to have called in the commander of his theater Army Air Corps and told him to "keep the Japanese air forces out of my way." That was the only order issued and the subordinate was left free to decide how he would accomplish the mission. Similarly, commanders operating far from their superiors have historically been required to operate on mission orders–Hannibal crossing the Alps and British fleet commanders during the Age of Sail come to mind almost immediately. However, such cases of control-free C2 have been relatively rare in history and very rare since the telegraph and wireless made it possible for senior commanders to stay in touch. Indeed, the Israeli forces explicitly chose to adopt an interventionist approach despite their sense that the World War II German model was the most successful historically precisely because they feared loss of control in key engagements.

Self-Synchronization

That same concern has been expressed by many of those who examine the NCW tenets stating that self-synchronized forces and actions will be enabled, both within the U.S. and among our coalition partners. However, the assumptions for self-synchronization[18] make it clear that the result will not be chaos in the battlespace. They are:

- Clear and consistent understanding of command intent;

- High quality information and shared situational awareness;

- Competence at all levels of the force; and

- Trust in the information, subordinates, superiors, peers, and equipment.

The command function is not absent in self-synchronized forces; however, it does depend on achieving congruent command intent, shared situation awareness, authoritative resource allocation, and appropriate rules of engagement, as well as similar measures that guide but do not dictate details to subordinates.

Moreover, the tenets of NCW do not assume that self-synchronization is the only way Information Age forces will operate. They argue only that they will be capable of such operations and that those operations will be more effective (greater likelihood of mission accomplishment) and efficient (few forces able to do more). Unless the conditions necessary for self-synchronized operations are met, there is no assumption that it should be employed.

The Battle of Trafalgar (1805)

The argument is often made that nothing genuinely new ever occurs in warfare, just as the argument is made that every engagement, battle, campaign, and war is new and different. Looking at the history of warfare, the British fleet in the Battle of Trafalgar appears to be a genuine example of self-synchronized forces. It has the key characteristics of such a force:

- Clear command intent from Admiral Lord Nelson;

- Competence among the decisionmakers (ship captains);

- Rich, shared information about the battlespace; and

- Trust between commanders at all levels.

The self-synchronization began well before the first shot was fired. Lord Nelson was known as a brave, innovative, and creative commander. He was entrusted with the main battle fleet and given the mission of finding and destroying the combined Spanish and French battle fleet. He actually sailed from English waters to the West Indies in search of his adversary before locating them in waters off the Spanish coast.[19]

The traditional way for naval fleet battles to be conducted at this time was to form a "line of battle" and sail parallel with the enemy's line, exchanging fire, often at close range. At times, the decisive combat came when two vessels came together and hand to hand fighting ensued between the crews. The English fleet knew that it had some very real disadvantages in this scheme of warfare–the Spanish and French vessels were typically heavier and carried more guns, which meant that they had a real advantage in "weight of metal," the amount of shot that could be delivered in a single broadside.

At the same time, the English also knew they had some advantages. Their vessels were lighter, but were also captained and crewed by more highly skilled sailors and were much more maneuverable than their adversaries, particularly under fire. They also knew that they had better trained gun crews, which translated into being able to fire more often and more accurately than the Spanish and French ships.

Lord Nelson decided that his goal should be to neutralize the advantages of his enemy by refusing to slug it out, toe to toe. Instead, he was willing to risk his vessels by attacking perpendicularly to the enemy's line (Figure 1). This meant exposing his vessels' lightly armed bows to the full broadsides of the French and Spanish. However, if his ships could break the line, they would be able to deliver their own broadsides into the stern of one vessel and/or the bow of another. His expectation was that this tactic would break the formation of the enemy and turn the battle into a series of ship-to-ship engagements where his forces' greater maneuverability, higher rate of fire, and capacity to work together would prove decisive.[20]

This was a risky approach that depended on excellent handling of the British ships so that they would be able to time their initial attack to sail between enemy ships (reducing the number of guns that could be brought to bear on them as they approached the battle line) and deliver a devastating first blow. Similarly, it assumed that the British captains would carry the subsequent attack to the enemy with vigor and would support one another when dealing with the heavier enemy vessels.

Nelson was careful to discuss this approach with his captains in a series of meetings that he called aboard his flagship as the battle fleet formed, crossed the Atlantic, and returned. This included discussions with Admiral Collingwood, whose force

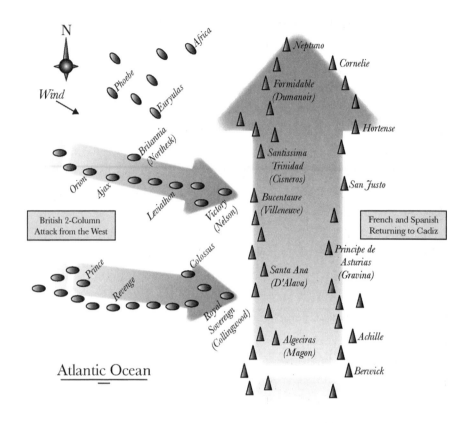

N

Wind

Africa

Phoebe

Euryalus

Britannia (Northesk)

Orion

Ajax

Leviathon

Victory (Nelson)

British 2-Column Attack from the West

Prince

Revenge

Colossus

Royal Sovereign (Collingwood)

Atlantic Ocean

Neptuno

Cornelie

Formidable (Dumanoir)

Hortense

Santissima Trinidad (Cisneros)

San Justo

Bucentaure (Villeneuve)

French and Spanish Returning to Cadiz

Principe de Asturias (Gravina)

Santa Ana (D'Alava)

Algeciras (Magon)

Achille

Berwick

Figure 1. Nelson's Innovation at the Battle of Trafalgar

joined Nelson about three weeks before the battle. The discussion focused on naval warfare tactics first introduced by George Brydges Rodney, a British captain who defended the Bahamas from the French in 1782 using the broken line tactics that Nelson would employ nearly 20 years later.[21] There was a major conference aboard Nelson's flagship, HMS *Victory*, the night before the battle, but this was largely an affirmation of the tactics to be used, ensuring that each captain knew where his ship would be in the initial attack formation.

Once the battle was joined there was little or no opportunity for communications between the British captains. Even so, the battle was conducted with skill and effectiveness. Nelson was able to gain the "weather gage" with the wind favoring his fleet. Both of the attacking columns and most of the ships within them were able to approach the Spanish and French line of battle without suffering from more than one broadside. Many of them were able to deliver their first broadside into the bow or stern of at least one enemy vessel, wreaking havoc as their fire traversed the length of the enemy's decks.

The English advantages proved decisive. First, the somewhat lighter British ships were largely able to avoid a "battle of broadsides" using their greater maneuverability to position themselves at angles where more of their guns could bear and they were firing down the length of the Spanish and French ships. Second, the British captains supported one another effectively. Several times during the fight, an English ship that had already engaged a larger foe was joined by another English ship attacking the enemy vessel from the opposite side.[22] Since the French and Spanish had relatively few qualified gunners, they were at a very real disadvantage when having to fight from both sides of the ship. Their fire became less accurate and even slower when forced to split their qualified cadre of gunners.

The result of the British capability to self-synchronize in the battle was a major victory. While most of the English vessels suffered some damage and Lord Nelson was killed, not a single vessel was lost during the battle. By contrast, the combined French and Spanish fleet lost some 20 vessels[23] to capture, explosion, fire, and scuttling.

COMMAND AND CONTROL APPROACHES IN THE INFORMATION AGE

Given a robustly networked force, any one of the six effective command and control philosophies proven useful in the Industrial Age is possible. That is, the communications systems will exist to centralize C2 almost completely and follow either a cyclic philosophy or, more likely, an interventionist one. At the same time, the distribution of information will allow use of a control-free or selective control approach when they are more appropriate. Objective-based C2 will be an included case. Hence, the criteria for selecting the proper approach will depend on factors other than the reach, richness, and quality of service of the U.S. network. Put another way, our organizations, architectures, and systems will no longer constrain the way that we accomplish command and control.

First, where a robustly networked, highly professional force exists, whether that is U.S.-only or a coalition force, and the battlespace is dynamic (changing rapidly), self-synchronization (read control-free) appears attractive. However, in order to work together effectively in this mode, the elements of this force will have to achieve a high level of trust. At a minimum, this means that they must have exercised together successfully across the range of missions involved. Forums such as NATO and regular bilateral exercises such as those PACOM participates in around the Pacific Rim are the types of efforts that are required. More ideally (though less desirable in that they imply that the U.S. is engaged in combat operations), they will have operated together in that mission space. In a very real way, the multinational special operations forces that cooperated successfully in Afghanistan represent this model. Many of them had trained together in NATO or bilateral exercises and some of them had operated together over the preceding years. They represented highly competent forces and were able to share detailed tactical information relevant to the mission.

In circumstances where the necessary experience and trust have not been developed, but the professionalism and creativity of the force is not in question, mission orders and selective control may be the desired approach. By maintaining a central headquarters with the authority to intervene to take advantage of major opportunities or threats that none of the component commands can deal with effectively, the flexibility and innovation inherent in mission orders can be retained while the mechanism to develop, monitor, and maintain a match between command intent and the best use of the force is created at the theater level.

Where the force contains elements with seriously different doctrines and approaches to the missions at hand and the battlespace is likely to be dynamic, the objective-oriented approaches may be more relevant. In these cases, the time honored ways of controlling very different forces–physical partition of the battlespace, creation of a central military command that is staffed by representatives of all the military forces involved, exchange of liaison officers, plans that deconflict and synchronize actions–may be important. This is particularly true if the operations are to be synergistic.

C2 philosophies that depend on orders from the center may also be important in the Information Age. First, when part of the force has doctrine that requires orders from the center (true today in many Third World militaries that may be part of a coalition of the willing, even a desirable part in terms of global support or cultural interface), some mechanism must exist to provide those orders. Second, when part of the force lacks the professional competence to contribute to the mission independently, centralized orders may be necessary. Perhaps most important during crises (where a misstep can lead to war, where quality decisionmaking will control the situation short of war) or when decisionmaking about weapons of mass effects are involved, centralized control may be desirable.

Three challenges are inherent in this formulation:

- First, the network and supporting elements of U.S. mission capability packages must be developed and assessed in terms of their ability to support the spectrum of C2 philosophies, not just one point in that spectrum.

- Second, U.S. personnel, particularly decisionmakers, must understand the different approaches, the circumstances where they apply, and how they can be implemented effectively across that range of circumstances.

- Third, those responsible for the command function must have the skills and insight to guide the force across the full spectrum of C2 approaches.

These challenges represent a major departure from the C2 practices of the Industrial Age. The comfortable position of selecting a single philosophy and working to establish it in doctrine and training is disappearing as we move into the Information Age.

NOTES

1   Alberts, David S. and Richard E. Hayes. *Command Arrangements for Peace Operations*. Washington, DC: CCRP Publication Series. p. 5.

2   Jomini, General Baron Antione Henri. "The Command of Armies and the Supreme Control of Operations." *Precis de l'Art de Guerre.* Chapter 2. Article 14. 1838.
Jomini, Antione Henri. *The Art of War.* New York, NY: Greenhill Press. 1996.

3   Clausewitz, Carl von. Michael E. Howard and Peter Paret, eds. *On War.* Princeton, NJ: Princeton University Press. 1976.

4   Department of Defense Dictionary of Military and Associated Terms. Joint Pubs. 1-02.
http://www.dtic.mil/doctrine/jel/doddict/. (Apr 1, 2003)

5   Alberts, *Command Arrangements.* pp. 7-13.

6   Alberts, *Understanding.* p. 142-3.

7   A more detailed discussion of both the traditional view of the command and control process and an Information Age view of these processes can be found in: Alberts, *Understanding.* pp. 131-184.

8   Verkerk, Maarten J., Jan De Leede, and Andre H.J. Nijhof. "From Responsible Management to Responsible Organizations: The Democratic Principle for Managing Organizational Ethics." *Business and Society Review.* New York, NY. Winter 2001.
Bragg, Terry. "Ten Ways to Deal with Conflict." *IIE Solutions.* Norcross. Oct 1999.
Bushardt, Stephen C., David L. Duhon, and Aubrey R. Fowler, Jr. "Management Delegation Myths and the Paradox of Task Assignment." *Business Horizons.* Greenwich. Mar/Apr 1991.

9   Pigeau, Ross, and Carol McCann. "Re-conceptualizing Command and Control." *Canadian Military Journal.* Vol 3, No 1. Spring 2002.

10   Ibid, p.57.

11   Alberts, *Understanding.* pp. 142-3.

12   Alberts, *Command Arrangements.* pp. 77-100.
Alberts, *Understanding.* pp. 169-180.

13   Glantz, David M. *The Role of Soviet Intelligence in Soviet Military Strategy in WWII.* Novato, CA: Presidio Press. 1990.

14   Rice, Condoleezza. "The Party, the Military, and Decision Authority in the Soviet Union." *World Politics.* Vol. 40, No. 1. October 1987. pp. 55-81.

15   Defense Systems, Inc. *Headquarters Effectiveness Program Summary Task 002.* Arlington, VA: C3 Architecture and Mission Analysis, Planning and Systems Integration Directorate, Defense Communications Agency. 1983.

16 Ibid.

17 Hughes, Wayne P. *Fleet Tactics - Theory and Practice*. Annapolis, MD: Naval Institute Press. 1986.

18 Some current military parlance employs the term *self-coordination* in place of self-synchronization. The DoD Transformational Planning Guidance issued in April 2003 defines self-coordination as an effort to "increase freedom of low level forces to operate near-autonomously and re-task themselves through exploitation of shared awareness and commander's intent." This definition is consistent with our concept of self-synchronization. Rumsfeld, Donald H. *Transformational Planning Guidance*. Department of Defense. April 2003.

19 "Nelson, Horatio Nelson, Viscount, Duke of Bronte in Sicily." © JM Dent/Historybookshop.com. http://www.phoenixpress.co.uk/articles/people/soldiers-military/nelson-pp.asp. (Apr 1, 2003)

20 "The Nelson Touch." The Nelson Society. Portsmouth, UK. 2001. http://www.nelson-society.org.uk/html/nelsons_touch.htm. (Apr 1, 2003)

21 "Battle of Trafalgar." Wikipedia: The Free Encyclopedia. Jan 3, 2003. http://www.wikipedia.org/wiki/Battle_of_Trafalgar. (Apr 1, 2003)

22 "The Battle." The Nelson Society. Portsmouth, UK. 2001. http://www.nelson-society.org.uk/html/battle_of_trafalgar.htm. (Apr 1, 2003)

23 "Trafalgar, Battle of." Microsoft® Encarta® Online Encyclopedia 2003. http://encarta.msn.com. (Apr 1, 2003) © 1997-2003 Microsoft Corporation. All Rights Reserved.

Chapter 3

Industrial Age C2

INDUSTRIAL AGE COMMAND AND CONTROL

Most of the existing philosophy, doctrine, and practice of command and control (C2) were developed and perfected during (and thus reflect) the Industrial Age.[1] The principles underlying traditional command and control apply not only to Industrial Age warfare, but also to Industrial Age economies and businesses. These principles are decomposition, specialization, hierarchy, optimization, deconfliction, centralized planning, and decentralized execution. Taken together, they create a pattern analogous to control theory.

Each of these principles and their implications are discussed briefly below. Note that they remain important elements in today's military organizations, both in the United States and in other nations. Also note that vanguard organizations and emerging social environments and commercial marketplaces are creating new rules governing relationships and developing new management approaches that differ significantly from the principles discussed below. These are discussed in the chapter that follows.

DECOMPOSITION

The Industrial Age applied a "divide and conquer" mentality to all problems. Academic disciplines, businesses, associations, and military organizations defined their roles as precisely as possible and divided their overall activities into coherent subsets that could be mastered with the existing knowledge, technologies, and personnel. Businesses looked to become horizontal and vertical monopolies by linking together selected chains of activities. Universities were divided into departments based on narrow discipline boundaries. Even today, many nongovernmental relief organizations work only within very narrow boundaries to provide food, water, medicine, education, or other specific services to specific populations. Similarly, the United Nations and other international organizations are divided into suborganizations with narrowly defined purposes.

Military organizations that developed during the Industrial Age also reflect the Industrial Age principle of decomposition. For example, the historical military staff functions (personnel, intelligence, operations, logistics, etc.) allow a commander to maintain a coherent grasp of the battlespace while the staff sections monitor, understand, report about, plan for, and implement functional activities within their areas of competence. Similarly, the practices of separating combat into land, sea, and air (and space), assigning physical areas of responsibility (AOR) to particular military organizations, and having different organizations responsible for fires and maneuver are other examples of decomposing warfare into manageable pieces. These pieces come together into a coherent whole in an Industrial Age military organization because they are integrated by planning done by or in the name of commanders. Even the command role is carved out of the overall military problem as a separate activity.

SPECIALIZATION

If a sound set of decompositions is made, then these organizational subsets of the organization (again, a business, bureaucracy, or military organization) can develop professional specialties that help the overall organization or enterprise to perform its mission and achieve its objectives. Individuals and specific elements of the organizational subsets (teams, groups, divisions, departments, agencies, etc.) are able to master their individual arts and sciences so as to competently employ their specialties in support of the larger organization. For example, drug manufacturers are divided into organizational entities responsible for research and development of new products, clinical trials, manufacturing, marketing, distribution, and supporting organizational structures such as accounting, legal, and information systems. The staffs of these segments each have very different training, skills, and organizational cultures. They each depend on a different set of specialists.

The Industrial Age raised specialization to heights not previously contemplated. The whole idea of an assembly line[2] in which a set of carefully sequenced actions generates enormous efficiency was unthinkable before this era. Academic disciplines also fractured into very narrow specialties, a fact reflected in the massive growth in professional journals–from dozens in the 17th century to hundreds in the 19th century, and thousands in the 20th (with tens of thousands worldwide by the end of that century). As professions developed over time, they also fractured into increasingly narrow specialties–medicine (geriatrics, gynecology, hematology), law (tax, intellectual property, environmental), and accounting (mergers and acquisitions, international, entertainment) are obvious examples.

In military affairs, specialization (creation of career branches and very specialized organizations) enabled much more efficient career development and training. During military operations, the specialized capabilities often generated capacities that simply could not be created by groups of generalists. For example, an integrated air operation involving intelligence about air defenses, detailed planning, command and control aircraft, tankers, escorts, electronic warfare aircraft, battle damage assessment, and support from search and rescue organizations would not be possible without highly specialized personnel, processes, organizations, and equipment.

Industrial Age militaries lack the quality of "jointness," the ability of individuals and organizations from multiple Services to work together synergistically. In Industrial Age militaries, various approaches were employed to help ensure that the activity of different Services were deconflicted, that they could operate on the battlefield without interfering with or harming each other. It was not until very recently, with the passage of Goldwater-Nichols[3] that a significant effort was made to make U.S. forces "joint." Until very recently, jointness was viewed as something that occurs at the operational (headquarters) level of command. This resulted in a continued lack of attention to creating the conditions for joint operations at the tactical level. Therefore, one could accurately characterize the Industrial Age approach to jointness as *joint planning*.

HIERARCHICAL ORGANIZATIONS

The organizational consequence of Industrial Age specialization is hierarchy. The efforts of individuals and highly specialized entities must be focused and controlled so that they act in concert to achieve the goals of the larger organizations or enterprises that they support. This implies the existence of a middle management layer of leaders whose tasks include:

- Understanding the overall goals and policies of the enterprise;

- Transmitting those goals to subordinates (and sometimes translating them into language the subordinates can understand and actions they can undertake);

- Developing plans to ensure coordinated actions consistent with the organization's goals and values;

- Monitoring the performance of the subordinates, providing corrective guidance when necessary; and

- Providing feedback about performance and changes in the operating environment to the leadership, and making recommendations about changes in goals, policies, and plans.

The size and the number of levels that separate the leader(s) of an enterprise and the specialists that are needed to accomplish the tasks at hand are a function of the overall size of the enterprise and the effective span of control, that is, how many individuals and/or organizational entities that can be managed by an individual or entity. Given that a hierarchy was needed to coordinate and integrate the activities of specialists and specialized organizations, the number of layers in the hierarchy then became a function of the effective span of control available.

In civilian organizations, the effective span of control was typically understood to be a dozen or less, some would argue as low as three to six.[4] Elliott Jaques,[5] James Wilson,[6] and Henry Mintzberg,[7] among others, discuss the need for multiple layers. These bureaucratic structures were intended to permit personal interfaces between the responsible manager and individuals at the next layer. As corporations, bureaucracies, and associations grew to enormous sizes, the number of middle managers and management layers grew as well. Examination of the organizational structures of government agencies, businesses, international organizations, and associations during the late 20th century shows that the proliferation of these middle managers was in response to a need to integrate and coordinate the activities of large hierarchical organizations.

Military hierarchies were also established on these same principles, but modified as necessary in response to the compelling need for clear and constant communications in the battlespace.[8] In ground combat, the organization of the U.S. Army illustrates the practical implications of these factors under the pressures of combat missions. That organization builds up its organizational entities from individuals to fire teams (5-6 individuals), squads (2 fire teams), platoons (up to 4 squads), companies (3-4 platoons), battalions (3-4 companies), brigades (3-4 battalions), divisions (3-4 brigades, with major subordinate organizations for fires [division artillery] and logistics), corps (3-4 divisions and major organizations for fires and logistics), and armies (3-4 corps). These same basic structures can be traced back to the Civil War when communications relied on voice of command, bugles, couriers, semaphore flags, and the telegraph. The massive size and number of layers within the Department of Defense is a reflection of this same practice. The number of layers is a function of the span of control. As the span of control decreases, the number of layers that are needed (for an organization of the same size) increases [9]

In such hierarchies, information needs to flow up and down the chain of command. This is true of policy information, plans, orders, and information about the battlespace (both reports about the enemy and reports about friendly forces). The more layers, the longer this takes and the higher the probability of an error or distortion. Even today, correspondence to a member of a military command is formally addressed to the commanding officer of the unit and is then distributed by the headquarters. In other words, all information intended for subordinates is recognized as belonging to and flowing through the hierarchy. Indeed, control of information was a major tool for controlling Industrial Age organizations.[10]

In military hierarchies, the commander's staff is often seen as the *control* mechanism, an adjunct to the *command* role of the formal leader or commander.[11] For example, Eisenhower's headquarters for OPERATION OVERLORD included more than 16,000 personnel.

OPTIMIZATION

Industrial Age militaries decomposed the battlespace, created layered organizations, divided into specializations, and organized forces into hierarchies. Thinking that this approach transformed the complexity of war and large operations into a collection of simple, manageable tasks and problems, the Industrial Age military felt that they were able to focus on the optimization of processes. A characteristic assumption of the Industrial Age was that every problem had a "best" solution and every asset had an ideal employment.[12] In the United States military, those assumptions were reinforced both by a national "can do" culture and the fact that engineering was the most common academic training for the professional officer corps (the U.S. Naval Academy at Annapolis began awarding a Bachelor of Science degree in 1933,[13] and the U.S. Military Academy at West Point, which originally taught only civil engineering, only offers a Bachelor of Science degree[14]). These assumptions naturally led to analyses seeking optimum solutions and patterns of employment. This was most obvious in the design of weapons systems that were optimized against the set of threats considered most likely and most dangerous to national interests. However, it was also obvious in the design of command and control systems and the communications systems intended to support them. Command and control also sought to create the optimum conditions for employing each type of unit or weapons platform—matching ends to means.

Until very recently, nation states could name the specific states or coalitions they considered their most likely and most dangerous adversaries. As a consequence, they felt that they could know the military forces they were most likely to fight and the terrain where the combat was most likely to occur. Many of the most important rivalries were characterized by arms races, often defined quantitatively in terms of the numbers of troops, cannon, or platforms that could be mobilized, the ranges of the weapons available to each side, or other factors that were perceived as providing competitive advantage.

For example, during the Cold War, the United States made all of its key decisions about force structure and weapons platforms with the Soviet Union, Warsaw Pact, and other Communist states in mind. Air Land Battle,[15] as an obvious example, was crafted as a way of defeating Soviet forces in the European theater. Virtually all Industrial Age militaries created "approved scenarios" against which their threat-based decisions were optimized. Of course, the difficulties they experienced when forced to fight against military organizations other than those they had planned against (the colonial powers in Wars of National Liberation, the U.S. in Vietnam, etc.) were partly a result of this assumption that force structures could be optimized and alternative warfighting contexts would be "lesser included cases."

DECONFLICTION

Given that the elements of military forces were optimized for specific missions under well known and understood circumstances, Industrial Age command and control processes relied heavily on control measures that would deconflict the elements of the force. These control measures included:

- Unit boundaries;

- Altitude restrictions on aircraft;

- Assignment of logistics facilities (road, rail, airfield, port) to particular organizations;

- No-fire zones, free fire zones, restrictions (need for clearance) on fires;

- Phase lines to coordinate movement;

- Rules of engagement, often linked to particular geographic areas; and

- Many, many others.

The goal here went beyond permitting military commanders to control what occurred in their areas of responsibility. While preventing unnecessary "friendly fire" and "collateral damage" was a priority, it was not the ultimate goal of physical deconfliction. The ultimate goal was to provide each element of the force with the best possible operating environment. This was a natural consequence of specialization and optimization. While combined arms operations (for example, infantry, armor, and artillery working together to attack an enemy position) were practiced by professional forces, they were largely organized by deconfliction. For example, this required ensuring that the artillery fire was coordinated in time and space to have maximum effect on the enemy without endangering friendly infantry or armor. As we have discussed elsewhere,[16] deconfliction is far better than conflicted operations (where friendly units impede one another), but it falls well short of the performance possible when military assets are employed synergistically.

CENTRALIZED PLANNING

Planning became a crucial part of Industrial Age command and control because it enabled commanders to arrange forces and events in time and space so as to maximize the likelihood of success (mission accomplishment). Military plans always include five elements:

- Missions–what is to be done by the overall force and each major element of that force (who is responsible for what);

- Assets–which parts of the force are assigned to each element of the mission (who plays what role);

- Boundaries–who has which areas of responsibility (what control measures are in force);

- Schedules–how the effort is organized over time; and

- Contingencies–how missions, assets, boundaries, and schedules will change under specific pre-identified circumstances.

Given the limits of Industrial Age communications, *plans* were the mechanisms by which military commanders sought to create the conditions necessary for success. Large, complex organizations in particular depended on comprehensive plans that required considerable time to prepare and also had to be continuously monitored, adjusted, and maintained. The classic U.S. Air Tasking Order (ATO), perfected during the last decades of the 20th century, is an excellent example of the detailed planning required to integrate and coordinate the actions of complex forces. That planning document could only be produced by the large headquarters of a numbered air force (thousands of specialized personnel). It required 72 hours to produce and implement, but it tasked every aircraft, by tail number, and provided the information necessary for them to work together.

DECENTRALIZED EXECUTION

Industrial Age commanders were, however, aware of the fragility of plans in the face of the harsh and dynamic operating environment of combat. Perhaps the most famous quotation about planning from that era (all the more relevant because it was uttered by one of the great planners in history) is, "No plan survives first contact with the enemy."[17] Understanding the limits of military plans, commanders (particularly in highly professional forces such as those of Germany during World War II or NATO) encouraged initiative (innovation and aggressive actions) and decentralized execution within the overall commander's intent. This was not just a concession to the inherent difficulty of foreseeing all eventualities. It was also a reflection of the fact that the commander on the scene often had better information than those removed from the battlespace.

Keegan discusses command and control as a continuous process of uncertainty reduction.[18] That process occurs very rapidly at the time and place where forces become engaged. Small fights inform engagements, which in turn inform battles, which ultimately inform campaigns. During the Industrial Age, the sensors and communications systems typically forced major decisions on the forward commander, who had to decide both how to implement the plan and also when it had become irrelevant or dysfunctional. The flexibility and innovation necessary for accomplishing the mission typically resided with those implementing the plans much more than with those developing them.[19]

INDUSTRIAL AGE C2–SIMPLE ADAPTIVE CONTROL MECHANISMS

Largely because of the limits of Industrial Age communications technologies, command and control systems developed during that era were inherently cyclical. That is, they monitored a battlespace situation (friendly, adversary, terrain, weather, etc.), generated situation awareness, fused the information at hand with their prior knowledge to gain an understanding of the military situation, generated alternatives to improve that situation, chose among the alternatives, created plans to implement the selected alternatives, generated and distributed directives that conveyed those plans to subordinates, and monitored their effect reinitiating the cycle. The popularity of the OODA loop (Observe, Orient, Decide, Act) among professional militaries is a reflection of their recognition of this cyclic process. [20]

Industrial Age military organizations use simple, often linear command and control mechanisms. That is, they decompose the battlespace, phase (decompose over time) their operations, use specialization, optimization, and centralized planning to make their actions efficient, and employ decentralized execution and cyclic processes to ensure that their efforts are flexible and responsive to the operating environment. Their goal is adaptive control–continual pressures to control selected features of the battlespace (casualty ratios, territorial control, etc.) by adjusting their actions as the situation changes. This is an important (but incomplete) step toward the agility needed by Information Age forces.

NOTES

1   Toffler, Alvin. *War and Anti-War.* Boston, MA: Warner Books. 1995.

2   McCollum, Sean. "America on Wheels." *Scholastic Update.* New York, NY. Feb 7, 1997.

3   *Goldwater Nichols Department of Defense Reorganization Act of 1986.* National Defense University. http://www.ndu.edu/library/goldnich/goldnich.html. (Mar 21, 2003)

4   "The nearer we approach the supreme head of the whole organization, the more we ought to work towards groups of three; the closer we get to the foot of the whole organization, the more we work towards groups of six." – Sir Ian Hamilton, British Army. *The Soul and Body of an Army.* Arnold, London. 1922. p. 229.
    Miller, G.A. "The magical number seven, plus or minus two: Some limits on our capacity for processing information." *The Psychological Review.* Vol 63. 1956. pp. 81-97.

5   Jaques, Elliott. *General Theory Bureaucracy.* Portsmouth, NH: Heinemann. 1981.

6   Wilson, James Q. *Bureaucracy: What Government Agencies Do and Why They Do It.* New York, NY: Basic Books. 1991.

7   Mintzberg, Henry. *Mintzberg on Management: Inside Our Strange World of Organizations.* New York, NY: The Free Press. 1988.

8   Creveld, Martin van. *Command in War.* Cambridge, MA: Harvard University Press. 1985.

9   Urwick, L.F. "The Manager's Span of Control." *Harvard Business Review.* Cambridge, MA: Harvard Business Press. May-June 1958.

10 Alberts, *Information Age Transformation.* p. 60.

11 Alberts, *Command Arrangements.* p. 7.

12 Even if one could optimize each of the pieces that resulted from a decomposition of the overall problem, the result may not be optimal for the overall problem. This depends upon the behavior of the variables and the nature of their inter-dependencies.

13 United States Naval Academy. History of the Academy. http://www.usna.edu/VirtualTour/150years/. (Feb 22, 2003)

14 United States Military Academy. History of the Academy. http://www.usma.edu/bicentennial/history/. (Feb 22, 2003)

15 Simpson, D. Richard. "Doctrine -Who Needs It? You Do!" *Mobility Forum.* Scott AFB. May/Jun 1998.

16 Alberts, *Understanding.* p. 205.

17 Helmuth Carl Bernard von Moltke (the Elder), 19th century Prussian Field Marshall.

18 Keegan, John. *The Mask of Command.* New York, NY: Viking Penguin. 1988.

19 Davenport, T.H. and Prusack, L. *Working Knowledge: How Organizations Manage What They Know.* Cambridge, MA: Harvard Business School Press. 1998.
Weick, K.E. and Sutcliffe, K.M. *Managing the Unexpected: Assuring High Performance in an Age of Complexity.* San Francisco, CA: Jossey-Wiley. 2001.

20 Hammonds, Keith H. "The Strategy of the Fighter Pilot." *Fast Company.* June 2002. p. 98.
http://www.fastcompany.com/online/59/pilot.html. (May 1, 2003)

Chapter 4

Breakdown of Industrial Age Organizing Principles and Processes

The 21st century national security environment differs qualitatively from the security environment that nations faced in the Industrial Age.[1] Militaries now need to respond to a wider range of potential threats, many that are difficult to assess and many that cannot be responded to with conventional military tactics and capabilities. Expectations regarding casualties and collateral damage have made it more important to deploy with greater information quality and precision. Many operations require that militaries work together with a variety of civil and nongovernmental partners. The net result is that military planners are faced with more uncertainty with regard to what they need to be prepared to do, a more complex set of tasks to accomplish, and less room for error.[2]

THE INDUSTRIAL AGE LEGACY

Industrial Age militaries are comfortable doing threat-based planning and focusing on traditional combat and combat skills. This is a result of the Industrial Age biases toward decomposition and specialization. Thus, they focus on a small fraction of today's mission space. Industrial Age militaries have become optimized for a small (and arguably less relevant) part of the mission spectrum. Recently, the U.S. has shifted from threat-based to capability-based planning, in part to avoid this narrow focus.[3]

Industrial militaries have practiced working together, but only on a specialty-to-specialty basis. It has been said that the U.S. Navy is more comfortable working with the British Navy than with the U.S. Army. Whether this is true is debatable, but there is much evidence that cross-specialty and cross-cultural collaboration is difficult.[4] Certainly it has been difficult in peace operations for military and humanitarian organizations to work well together.[5]

Industrial Age militaries have, as a result of their size, the way they are organized, and their approach to command and control, developed a "battle rhythm" that cannot easily be changed. Yet many of today's missions may require a faster speed of command than is typical of these work processes. The emergence of instant, 24-hour-a-day news programming also creates the need for changes in the normal battle rhythm for meeting with reporters to comment on developments. For example, events taking place in different time zones have created opportunities for adversaries to "spin" events without a timely U.S. or Allied response.[6] As a result, we were forced to develop a "24/7" information organization to deal with this situation. This is the military version of a virtual organization, very much like the virtual help desks, or virtual software development organization used by Information Age organizations in the private sector.

Faced with the breakdown of traditional processes, Industrial Age militaries have responded in a number of ways. In most instances, these responses have been to tinker with existing organizations and processes rather than to undertake more revolutionary change. Industrial Age militaries have initially responded to a recognition of the broadening of the military mission spectrum with the argument that traditional military organizations, processes, and skills were suitable for the rigors of combat and hence they would work adequately for "less stressful" missions. As it has become clear that virtually all significant military operations are coalition operations, their initial response was that agreement on a single (unified) chain of command was necessary. As it became clear that military operations would no longer be strictly military, that they would involve significant civil aspects or indeed become subordinated to civil agendas, militaries initially responded by trying to employ the Industrial Age principles of decomposition and deconfliction. Hence they have created civil-military information centers (CIMICs) and civil-military operations centers (CMOCs) as specialized organizations outside the normal functional structures to deal with the nonmilitary actors.[7] As it became clear that the speed of command of Industrial Age militaries was not sufficient to respond to more agile adversaries, the initial response was to develop one-time workarounds. Finally, as it has become clear that the failure to be adequately forewarned of the events of September 11, 2001, was a result of a lack of information sharing and analytic synthesis, and the initial response has been to create special organizations to bring it all together.

All of these initial responses share one thing in common; they rely on Industrial Age assumptions with respect to the nature of work processes, organization, and command and control. Because of the complexity of the security challenges faced, modern militaries need to (1) bring all of their information to bear to make sense of the situation and (2) be able to employ all of their assets to effectively respond to the situation. The Industrial Age principles and practices of decomposition, specialization, hierarchy, optimization, and deconfliction, combined with Industrial Age command and control based on centralized planning and decentralized execution, will not permit an organization to bring all of its information (and expertise) or its assets to bear. In addition, Industrial Age organizations are not optimized for interoperability or agility. Thus, solutions based upon Industrial Age assumptions and practices will break down and fail in the Information Age. This will happen no matter how well intentioned, hardworking, or dedicated the leadership and the force are.

Two key force capabilities needed by Information Age militaries are *interoperability* and *agility*. Organizations that are products of Industrial Age thinking are not well suited for significant improvements in interoperability or agility.

INTEROPERABILITY AND INDUSTRIAL AGE ORGANIZATIONS

As discussed in the previous chapter, Industrial Age military organizations have evolved into many-layered hierarchies populated with stovepiped organizations and centralized planning processes. Organizational entities that are not in the same stovepipe do not share information, nor do they normally work with one another. The systems they acquire independently are not designed to work together and are often optimized for existing processes and information exchange requirements. Furthermore, individuals and organizational entities with Industrial Age mindsets do not see a compelling need for interoperability. Instead they think it is more important that they or their organization configure their systems and processes to optimize the tasks for which they are responsible.

This behavior makes sense if one believes that the whole is a simple sum of its parts. If this is true, then little or no interactions need to take place across specialized entities. In Industrial Age organizations, it is assumed that if any synergies are required, the plan will account for them.

This places an enormous reliance on centralized planning. Centralized planning is a logical consequence of the application of Industrial Age principles and the state of the art of communications and computing in the Industrial Age. But centralized planning does not work well when faced with very dynamic and complex situations. Centralized planning does not work well in a coalition environment where the participants have overlapping objectives but different priorities, perspectives, and constraints.[8]

Until recently, militaries felt that interoperability did not matter as much as other capabilities. In the United States, it was not until the passing of Goldwater-Nichols[9] that a serious effort was made to encourage the separate Services to be more interoperable and work together in the battlespace.

Joint Vision 2010[10] increased the emphasis on jointness. But despite the efforts of senior leadership in militaries around the world to promote jointness and interoperability, stovepipes predominate in military organizations and coalitions assembled for missions, despite the enormous advances in information technologies that are bringing down the costs of interoperability.

The problem is one of a lingering Industrial Age mindsets, cultures, and norms of behavior. It has to do with the reward and incentive structures, loyalties, and the nature of the interactions among individuals and organizational entities. Organizations that continue to believe that they can successfully deal with problems by decomposing them, and that centralized planning will account for any synergies required to meet the challenges faced, will not value interoperability.

With the Information Age came a new and potentially powerful tool of warfare that has recently become known as Information Operations.[11] As one would expect, this tool was and is for the most part still being developed by a small, stovepiped community. Yet its value in battle will come from our ability to integrate the effects we can achieve in the information and cognitive domains with effects in the physical domain. This will not be possible given current organizations, doctrine, systems, and culture. Indeed, most military organizations continue to see Information Operations as a separate function that is managed outside the traditional operations organization. The effort in Iraq, ongoing at this writing, may be an example of better integration of these efforts.

Fortunately, we have for the most part progressed to the point where most people recognize that more sharing of information and more collaboration are necessary. It is necessary to make sense of the increasingly complex situations we face. It is necessary to work with others who have different assumptions and different understandings. It is necessary to be able to orchestrate the various means at our disposal in an effective and timely manner.

However, the approach that many take to interoperability remains rooted in Industrial Age thinking. This Industrial Age approach to interoperability is based on the belief that it is possible to specify the information exchanges and collaborations that are needed in advance. It is hard for many to accept that this is not amenable to analysis, and that therefore it is not possible to know who may need what piece of information, when it will be needed, and who may need to work with whom. Being able to "divide and conquer" a problem was the hallmark of the Industrial Age, whether or not this was ever really possible.

The result is that, as some have put it, "everyone needs to talk to everyone." We would put it a slightly different way. Since one cannot know who will need to work with our systems and processes, they should not be designed to make it difficult to do so. On the contrary, they must be built to support a rich array of connectivity to be agile. The same is true with our processes. They need to be adaptable in terms of who participates as well as who plays what roles.

AGILITY AND THE INDUSTRIAL AGE

Industrial Age organizations are, by their very nature, anything but agile. Agile organizations must be able to meet unexpected challenges, to accomplish tasks in new ways, and to learn to accomplish new tasks. Agile organizations cannot be stymied when confronted by uncertainty or fall apart when some of their capabilities are interrupted or degraded. Agile organizations need to be able to tolerate (even embrace) disruptive innovation. Agile organizations depend upon the ability of individual members and organizational entities to get the information that they need to make sense of a situation and to combine and recombine as needed to ensure coherent responses. The lack of agility inherent in Industrial Age organizations is more than simply a result of a systemic lack of interoperability, although a lack of interoperability significantly impacts the agility of an organization. This lack of agility stems directly from an Industrial Age belief in optimization and centralized planning.

Optimization assumes a fair amount of knowledge about the nature of the response surface involved. A response surface consists of points, each of which reflects the value of an option given a certain situation or state (set of values for the independent variables that characterize the situation). An example of a response surface is depicted in Figure 2. Optimization is a process that seeks to find a solution (a military option, organizational form, process, system design) that gives the best possible result, a global maximum, as depicted in Figure 3. Optimization inherently involves tradeoffs. Given a choice between an option that yields the best result (the global optimum) and another option that may not be as good as the global optimum, but maintains its value over a larger range of conditions, Industrial Age organizations systemically have chosen to go with the global optimum. This is because these involve very narrowly framed decisions taken by specialists. The complexity and

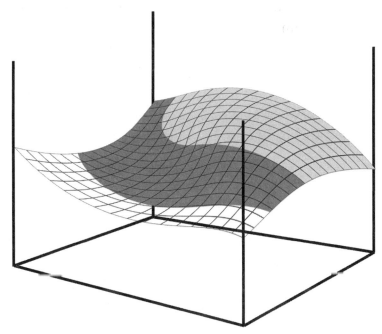

Figure 2. Sample Response Surface

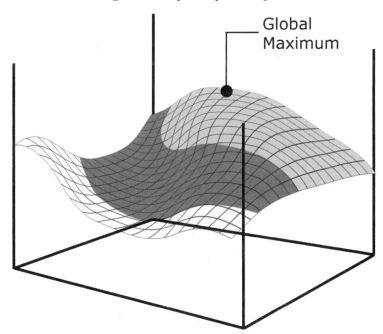

Figure 3. Location of the Global Maximum

uncertainty inherent in real world situations has been systematically forced out of consideration by the decomposition of the mission and the force.

This fixation on optimality often results in the selection of an option that sacrifices agility in the hopes of achieving the best possible result in the current case. For example, such options include the selection of a military option that will work if an adversary does what is expected, a network that has only the links that are expected to be used, or a process that restricts participation, but is fast. When things go right, they go very right. When things do not go as anticipated, they may not work at all. This form of gambling is not a good bet in the Information Age because of the range of relevant situations, their dynamics and complexity, as well as the uncertainties inherent in them.

Centralized planning is a manifestation of a belief in the ability to optimize. For centralized planning to work, it must be possible for a relatively small group of people to do all of the following: make sense of the situation, maintain this understanding in the face of a dynamic environment, predict the future, develop an appropriate response strategy, decompose the response into a coherent set of executable tasks, allocate resources, task subordinates, monitor execution, and make adjustments as required, all in a timely manner. In fact, despite a belief in the power of reductionism and a strong desire to optimize, centralized planning has evolved into a set of processes that often prevent optimization. Ironically, centralized planning processes are designed to deconflict tasks and elements of the force so that they will not get in each other's way or do harm to one another. *They prize deconfliction over synergy.* This prevents simultaneity and the synergies necessary to perform anywhere near optimality. Centralized planning is antithetical to agility because it (1) is relatively slow to recognize and respond to changes in the situation, (2) results in ill-informed participants, and (3) places many constraints on behavior.

INFORMATION AND INDUSTRIAL AGE ORGANIZATIONS

The inability of Industrial Age organizations to compete in the Information Age is a result of the way they deal with information. More to the point, they do not effectively take advantage of the information and expertise that are available. An organization that does not promote the widespread sharing of information will not have well informed individuals and organizational entities. An organization that develops an approach to command and control that takes full advantage of the information available will be at a competitive advantage.[12]

Industrial Age organizations create fixed seams through which information is lost. They create seams that prevent information from being brought to bear. And they create seams that prevent them from integrating effects. These organizations will survive only as long as it takes for others in their competitive space to take advantage of Information Age concepts and technologies. This will not be long.

The hierarchies that developed out of the Industrial Age often exhibit dysfunctional behaviors that are a result of the misalignment of responsibility and authority and/or a lack of appropriate accountability, despite the "common wisdom" that hierarchies are needed to clarify who is responsible and "where the buck stops." Although there are many reasons for the documented failures to properly allocate responsibility and to match responsibility with authority in the very organization thought to be a paragon of hierarchy (the military),[13] systemic problems result from the seams that are created by stovepipes (seams between and among functions and Services). These seams create gaps in roles and responsibilities that lead to a lack of accountability for interoperability, information sharing, and collaboration, all of which are necessary for a transformed military. These are failures related more to inaction rather than to taking the wrong action. They are often failures related to making suboptimal decisions rather than sacrificing locally for the good of the larger organization or mission. As such, they are hard to deal with in traditional military hierarchies.

A TALE OF TWO CORPORALS

Perhaps nothing makes the difference between Industrial Age Warfare and Information Age Warfare clearer than the roles attributed to army corporals from those two eras–Napoleon's Corporal and the Strategic Corporal (Figure 4).

Napoleon's Corporal was said to be on call within the Emperor's headquarters, day or night. His role was to listen to Napoleon's draft orders before they were sent to the generals. When the orders had been crafted so clearly that even the corporal could not misunderstand them, then they were considered ready for dissemination. In a sense, this was a version of the more modern KISS principle, "Keep it simple, stupid." Of course, this practice implied that Napoleon's Corporal was not an intellectual giant and would be easily confused by subtle or nuanced directives, and that orders had to be crafted so they were very difficult to misconstrue.

Figure 4. Napoleon's Corporal (left)[14] *and the Strategic Corporal (right)*[15]

By contrast, the Strategic Corporal is a creature of the Information Age. This is a junior noncommissioned officer who must be able to function across a range of missions and make decisions that have implications far beyond his local responsibilities. For example, the Strategic Corporal might be responsible for a roadblock late at night during a peace operation. He (or increasingly, she) may have to decide what to do about a civilian vehicle that approaches the roadblock at a high rate of speed and does not appear to intend to stop. If the occupants are innocent civilians, then firing on the vehicle may result in casualties (and very unfavorable media reporting) and a serious loss of trust among the local population. However, if the occupants are hostiles, then failure to stop it may result in an attack on his unit, a later violent event (bombing or assassination), or the loss of control over the road. The corporal must make his decision based on his situation awareness (Have there been similar incidents? What kind of vehicle is it? What types of occupants does it appear to contain?), his orders, the rules of engagement, and his judgment or common sense.

General Charles Krulak (USMC) set the stage for the importance of the flexibility and innovation required from the Strategic Corporal when he discussed the need to fight the "three block war." He stated that,

> *"in one moment in time, our service members will be feeding and clothing displaced refugees - providing humanitarian assistance. In the next moment, they will be holding two warring tribes apart - conducting peacekeeping operations. Finally, they will be fighting a highly lethal mid-intensity battle. All on the same day, all within three city blocks. It will be what we call the three block war."*[16]

Given the situations in Afghanistan and Iraq at this writing, this description seems prescient. The flexibility, innovation, and adaptability required by all elements of such a force to be effective across this range of contexts will place great demands on decisionmakers at all levels.

Two war stories from the recent past illustrate the very real capability of the junior non-commissioned officers in today's force and hold out great hope for the future. One comes from Canadian forces in Kosovo; the other is from U.S. forces in Haiti. Both stories reportedly have a basis in fact, though they may be changing as they are told and retold.

The Kosovo case occurred while small patrols were being sent out to search for weapons in villages that were supposed to be pacified. The Canadian troops had to request permission to enter houses that were almost exclusively populated by women. In order to search efficiently, the search teams used a small dog (a cocker spaniel) trained to detect explosives. At the first house, the non-commissioned officer leading the patrol asked the woman at the door if the troops might enter the house to look for weapons. She replied with a question, "Do you mean the weapons the army left with us and said they would come back for?" The soldier didn't miss a beat, immediately saying "yes." A number of weapons were found. For the rest of the patrol, the Canadian troops asked specifically about the weapons left by the army. At another house, the woman who answered the door offered to provide water for the dog. Once inside, the dog detected explosives and for the rest of the patrol, the troops always asked if the host would provide water for the dog.[17]

The other story tells of an American junior non-commissioned officer serving in Haiti who found himself responsible for security in a village because the political authorities (mayor, etc.) and the police authorities had disappeared when the regime changed. One afternoon, a highly agitated Haitian woman came running up to the soldier screaming and waving her arms. After several minutes and a variety of efforts to calm the woman, the interpreter reported that she was terrified because another villager had placed a curse on her, causing her and her family to shrink. The U.S. soldier listened to this and then reached for a pouch on his utility belt and pulled out a small envelope, which he tore open and scattered the contents (a brown powder) over the woman while chanting the Notre Dame fight song in a loud voice. The woman settled down and thanked him for removing the curse, rushing home to tell her family that the Americans had saved them. The bag contained powdered ground coffee.

Finally, as this was being written, an article appeared in the press about OPERATION IRAQI FREEDOM in which a "senior Air Force officer" was quoted as saying that during "the first few days, things were moving so fast that it was difficult to optimize the use of anything. There is a price to be paid for simultaneity."[18] In our terms, the prompt suboptimization that created the desired effects was clearly preferable to the slow, ponderous processes that sought to optimize the use of weapons systems and platforms. Agile C2 is gradually becoming a reality. Work processes and organizational structures need to be adapted to allow greater innovation and flexibility at all levels.

The Information Age force will require agility in all warfare domains, none more important than the cognitive and social domains. The Strategic Corporal must be recruited, trained, and empowered.

NOTES

1   Creveld, *Transformation*.

2   ABCA. *Coalition Operations Handbook*. American-British-Canadian-Australian Program. 2001.
    http://www.abca.hqda.pentagon.mil/Publications/COH/ABCA-COH.PDF. (May 1, 2003)
    Clark, W.K. *Waging Modern War*. New York, NY: Perseus Books. 2001.
    Pierce, L.G. and E.K. Bowman. "Cultural barriers to teamwork in a multinational coalition environment." *23rd Army Science Conference*. Orlando, FL. Dec 2-5, 2002.

3   Davis, Paul K. "Institutionalizing Planning for Adaptiveness." in Paul K.
    Davis, ed., *New Challenges for Defense Planning—Rethinking How Much Is Enough.*
    Santa Monica, CA: RAND, MR-400-RC. 1994c.

4   Katzenbach, Jon R. and Douglas K. Smith. *The Discipline of Teams: A
    Mindbook-Workbook for Delivering Small Group Performance.* New York, NY: John
    Wiley & Sons, Inc. 2001.

5   Wentz, *Bosnia.* p. 119.
    Wentz, *Kosovo.* p. 269.
    Davidson, Lisa Witzig, Margaret Daly Hayes, and James J. Landon.
    Humanitarian and Peace Operations: NGOs and the Military in the Interagency Process.
    Washington, DC: CCRP Publications Series. December 1996.

6   Wentz, *Bosnia.* p. 167.
    Wentz, *Kosovo.* p. 175.
    Siegel, Pascale Combelles. *Target Bosnia: Integrating Information Activities in Peace
    Operations.* NATO-Led Operations in Bosnia-Herzegovina. Washington,
    DC: CCRP Publication Series. 1998.

7   "CIMIC Reconstruction." *NATO Review.* Vol 49, No 1. Brussels, BEL:
    NATO. Spring 2001.
    http://www.nato.int/docu/review/2001/0101-06.htm. (Apr 1, 2003)
    Wentz, *Kosovo.* p. 269.
    Davidson, *Humanitarian.*
    Elmquist, Michael. "CIMIC in East Timor: An account of civil-military
    cooperation, coordination and collaboration in the early phases of the East
    Timor relief operation." UN Office for the Coordination of Humanitarian
    Affairs (OCHA). 1999.
    http://wwwnotes.reliefweb.int/files/rwdomino.nsf/
    4c6be8192aef259cc12564f500422b3c/
    313ad8c125d1212cc125684f004a48bd?OpenDocument. (Apr 1, 2003)

8   Alberts, *Command Arrangements.*
    Weick, K.E. & Sutcliffe, K.M. *Managing the Unexpected: Assuring High
    Performance in an Age of Complexity.* San Francisco, CA: Jossey-Wiley. 2001.
    Roberts, Nancy. "Coping with the Wicked Problems: The Case of
    Afghanistan." Jones, L., J. Guthrie, and P. Steane, eds. *International Public
    Management Reform: Lessons from Experience.* London, ENG: Elsevier. 2001.

9   Full text of hearings, reports, provisions, etc. are provided by the library at
    National Defense University. March 21, 2003.
    http://www.ndu.edu/library/goldnich/goldnich.html. (Apr 1, 2003)

10 Chairman of the Joint Chiefs of Staff. *Joint Vision 2010*. Washington, DC: Department of Defense, Joint Chiefs of Staff. 1996. p. 9.

11 The reference here is to the use of information in warfare. Similar language is sometimes used to refer to the arenas of psychological operations, media relationships, public diplomacy, and similar issues. These are included in (but constitute only a part of) Information Operations. *Information Warfare* is a term that preceded Information Operations and was popular in the mid-1990s.

12 Alberts, *Understanding*.

13 In [Pearl Harbor], there was such a marked failure to allocate responsibility in the case of the Fourteenth Naval District that Admiral Bloch testified he did not know whom the commander in chief would hold responsible in the event of shortcomings with respect to the condition and readiness of aircraft. Ferguson, Homer, and Owen Brewster. "Minority Pearl Harbor Report." Joint Committee on the Investigation of the Pearl Harbor Attack, Congress of the United States. Pursuant to S. Con. Res. 27. *Investigation of the Pearl Harbor Attack*. 79th Congress, 2nd Session. Washington, DC: Government Printing Office. 1946. p. 493ff. http://www.ibiblio.org/pha/pha/congress/part_0.html. (May 1, 2003)

14 Valentine Armouries. "Napoleonic uniform, 1807-1812 French Fusilier dress." Used with permission. http://www.varmouries.com/cloth/ccloth08.html. (Apr 1, 2003)

15 Garamone, Jim. "Army Tests Land Warrior for 21st Century Soldier." *American Forces Press Service*. Department of Defense DefenseLink. http://www.defenselink.mil/news/Sep1998/9809117b.jpg. (Apr 1, 2003)

16 Krulak, Charles. "The Strategic Corporal: Leadership in the Three Block War." *Marine Corps Gazette*. Vol 83, No 1. January 1999. pp. 18-22.

17 Hillier, Major General. Rick J. "Leadership Thoughts from Canada's Army: Follow Me." Keynote Address of the 7th International Command and Control Research and Technology Symposium. Quebec City, QC: Canada. September 16-20, 2002.

18 Graham, Bradley, and Vernon Loeb. "An Air War of Might, Coordination and Risks." *The Washington Post*. Apr 27, 2003. p. A01.

Chapter 5

The Information Age

E conomics and power are historically closely related. What distinguishes the Information Age from the Industrial Age are the economics of information and the nature of the power of information. With the coming of the Information Age, there is an opportunity to provide widespread access to information-related services and capabilities only dreamed about in previous eras. This increased access to information provides an opportunity to rethink the ways that we organize, manage, and control.

ECONOMICS OF INFORMATION

"Ages" are proclaimed when something happens to cause a discontinuity in multiple dimensions that affect civilization. While it could be argued that the advent of the telegraph or even the book itself were the first, faint indications of the Information Age, it is more commonly believed that an early (if not the first) proclamation of the Information Age was in the mid-1980s when authors John Naisbitt, Patricia Aburdene, Alvin Toffler, and Robert Russell began describing the decline of manufacturing and the proliferation of computers as the mark of a new economic era.[1] However, it was not until quite recently, when computing and communication technologies developed to the point that networking became practical, that we really did enter into the Information Age.[2]

Changes in the processes of value creation are at the core of broad-based discontinuities. As observed in *Understanding Information Age Warfare*,[3] it is the changes in the economics of information and the implications of these changes that have ushered in the Information Age. The simultaneous improvements in information richness, reach, and the quality of virtual interactions are decreasing the impediments to collective action by individuals or groups of individuals separated by distance and time, or divided by functional, organizational, or political boundaries. Changes in the economics of information are redefining the concept of information power.

THE POWER OF INFORMATION REDEFINED

Information is power. However, in recent years the meaning of this adage has been radically redefined. This redefinition lies at the heart of an ongoing Information Age transformation of society, politics, economics, and organizations. It makes edge organizations possible.

The original precept, *knowledge is power*,[4] conveyed the notion that an individual's worth was related to their possession of information. The more exclusivity associated with the possession, the more valuable the information. Hence, information was a commodity like any other commodity, whose value was related to scarcity. Individual and organizational behaviors reflected this value paradigm. Hoarding information and exploiting its scarcity have been the norm for some time. Although this value proposition has always been antithetical to productivity, antisharing and anticollaborative behaviors have long been tolerated. In fact, they were often the norm in hierarchical and bureaucratic organizations.

These behaviors can no longer be tolerated because the economics of information have changed. With the cost of information and its dissemination dropping dramatically, information has become a dominant factor in the value chain for almost every product or service. As the costs drop, so do the barriers to entry. Hence, competitors in many domains are seizing on the opportunity provided by "cheap" information and communications to redefine business processes and products.

These trends apply to the realm of national security as well. Information Age concepts and technologies are being adopted by peer, niche, and asymmetrical adversaries. The national security challenge is exacerbated by the exponential decrease in the size and cost of weapons of mass destruction and disruption, and the ever more transparent world of the 21st century.

The continuation of the antisharing and anticollaborative processes and behaviors in DoD that arose from Industrial Age practices can no longer be tolerated because they would give a competitive edge to adversaries of all sizes and capabilities. The argument that our traditional military adversaries (peer competitors) and allies are even more resistant to change than we are and will be slower to adapt misses the point of September 11, 2001. The point is that the security environment has forever changed and that this new security environment requires orders of magnitude faster "sensemaking" and responses. Furthermore, to make sense of the situation requires that we are able to quickly bring to bear (1) information from many sources, including new sources, (2) a wide variety of expertise and perspectives (to understand, filter, and integrate the available information and knowledge), and (3) synchronized effects over multiple domains.

This simply cannot be done without changing attitudes, behaviors, and processes, as well as greatly enhancing the information-related capabilities made available to those throughout an organization.

TECHNOLOGY ENABLERS OF POWER TO THE EDGE

The information revolution in progress is all about the amount of information richness and reach and the quality of interactions between and among entities that are possible as a result of advances in technology. The roles that entities can play in an endeavor depend on the natures of the interactions that can take place between and among the entities. The natures of these interactions that are practical to contemplate have everything to do with the economics of information. The economics of information depend, in large part, on the state of the art and practice of information technology. The latter half of the 20th century witnessed an explosion in information technologies that has fundamentally changed the way that geographically and temporally separated entities can interact.[5]

As technology advances and the cost of providing selected services decreases, the ability to communicate improves and the challenges related to information distribution change. We have gone from a time where geographically dispersed individuals could only communicate if they were smart in two ways and were synchronous in time and space to a time when they can communicate even if they are less knowledgeable and are asynchronous in time and space. With each new capability, the set of limiting factors governing information dissemination has been reduced.

Characteristics of Telephone Exchanges

This story[6] starts with the circuit-based communications capabilities of the 1970s. With almost universal market penetration, the telephone provided a way, at least theoretically, for anyone in the United States to talk to anyone else. Theoretically, because one still needed to know the phone number of the person with whom you wanted to talk. However, with the proper phone number in hand, people anywhere in the United States could talk to one another provided that they both were in close proximity to a phone at the same time. Thus, geographically dispersed individuals could communicate by voice provided they were in specific places at the same time. This form of communications therefore required that the individuals in question be synchronous in time and space.

Given this capability, there was now a way for anyone in the United States to communicate a notable piece of information to anyone else in the United States. However, three barriers needed to be overcome in order to do so. First, the information needed to be recognized as notable by the person acquiring it (the first of the "smarts"). Second, the person needed to know (or ascertain) who would find the information useful, and the phone number(s) of the individual(s) involved (the second of the "smarts"). Third, given that these conditions were met, the amount of time required to pass the information along depended upon how long it took for (1) one person to recognize the need, (2) one person to obtain the appropriate phone number(s), and (3) both individuals to become synchronous in time and space. Thus, to provide or exchange information via telephone, we needed to rely on a *smart smart push* approach to information dissemination. Smart smart push via telephone requires that the pusher understand what information is needed by whom, plus how to get it there, and when the other party will be available to receive it. This is a nontrivial set of requirements that is difficult if not impossible to meet as missions become less traditional and more complex. Figure 5 illustrates the capabilities of the telephone measured in terms of the three attributes of the information domain: reach, richness, and quality of interactions.[7]

Since the value or the importance of any given piece of information depends on its context and/or the situation, without an adequate understanding of the situation being faced by another entity, the entity in possession of the information cannot judge its potential value or urgency. This makes it a very tall order for someone to be smart about who needs what. To extend the argument beyond one entity to a large organization, such as DoD, no single individual or small group of individuals can possibly know even a small fraction of the situations currently or potentially affecting people throughout the enterprise. Thus, no matter how hard they try to understand, monitor, and empathize with others, the collectors or acquirers of information cannot know even a small fraction of the individuals that will find the information of interest, or even those individuals for whom the information is vital. An exten-

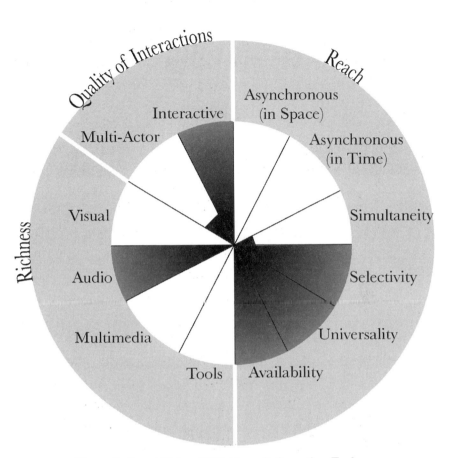

Figure 5. Capabilities of Telephone Information Exchange

sion of this argument reaches the conclusion that since each individual in each situation has a different need for information and can tolerate a different degree of ambiguity, the decision of what information to release cannot be left to the owner of the information. Actually, the concept of information *owners* is totally antithetical to Information Age thinking.

In the 1970s, information dissemination was limited by the ability (and willingness) of the owners of information to identify and know their customers. As a consequence, information was not distributed widely and its utility was constrained.

Rather, it was confined to selected organizational entities and their associated chains of command.

Characteristics of Broadcast Exchanges

In the late 1970s, the DoD acquired broadcast capabilities, moving from a point-to-point to a multicast capability. Thus, a person with information could broadcast it in the hopes that those that needed the information were listening. But this technology did not preserve or store information.[8] Thus, if someone was not listening at the moment of broadcast, the information perished. Of course, it could be broadcast again, but this only changed the probabilities a bit. From the listeners' point of view, there are many broadcasts on different channels. No one can pay attention to all broadcasts at all times. With broadcast, as with point-to-point methods of communication, one has to be synchronous in time (but not space) for information to be transferred. Figure 6 presents these capabilities and limitations. In broadcast mode, however, the individual wishing to convey information no longer needs to know the identity of the individuals or their phone number(s), and hence needs only one "smart." Thus, broadcast is smart push.

However, unlike a phone conversation, broadcast does not provide a confirmation of the receipt of the information. Of course, information possessors could use both the phone and a broadcast. Hence, the addition of a broadcast capability provides significant advantages, not the least of which is that many individuals could simultaneously receive intended information. Broadcast combined with the phone has helped people to provide their information to the right individuals at the right time. Thus, with only the telephone and broadcast

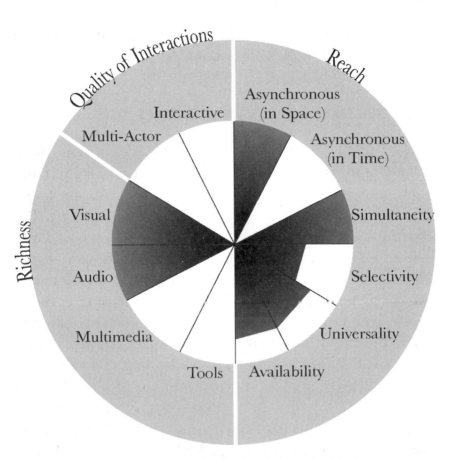

Figure 6. Capabilities of Broadcast Information Exchange

capabilities, information dissemination capabilities still leave much to be desired.

Characteristics of E-mail Exchanges

E-mail systems were introduced in the 1980s. Like a telephone, you still needed to know the address of the person you wish to communicate with (although there are some broadcast features available in some organizations that allow individuals to push a message to a selected group of individuals with some characteristic, such as membership in an organization, without needing to know their identities or addresses). The great advance that e-mail offers is that the two parties no longer need to be synchronous in time. And with the advent of wireless Personal Digital Assistants (PDAs, e.g. Blackberries), the parties no longer need to be synchronous in space (with respect to a fixed communications infrastructure). E-mail is not the same as a voice interaction. It does, however, have some significant advantages (Figure 7). It is persistent, indexable, and retrievable on demand.[9] It can carry context (the history of the conversation). E-mail can also be forwarded. But

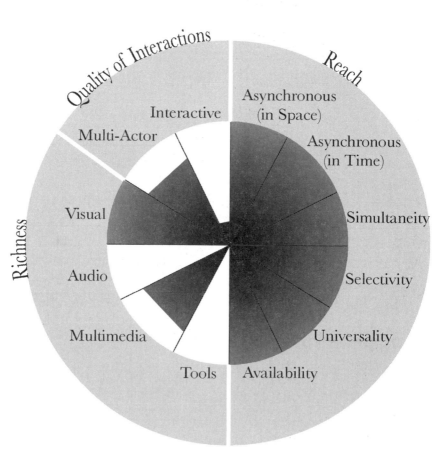

Figure 7. Capabilities of E-mail Information Exchange

of course, it does not allow users to get beyond the first two barriers to being able to effectively disseminate information (knowing what is important and who needs to know what).

Characteristics of a Networked Environment

The next stage in the evolution of information exchange technologies is the fully networked collaborative environment[10] (Figure 8). This environment, or suite of technologies, fully enables all of the attributes of reach, richness, and quality of

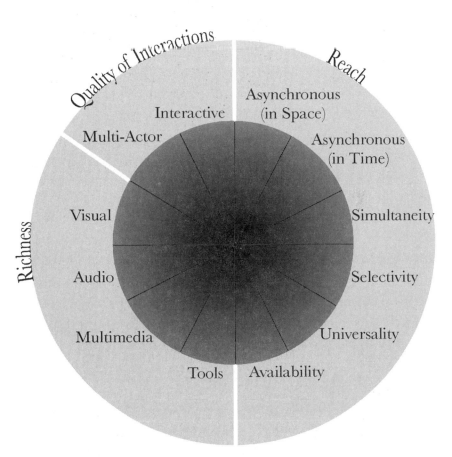

Figure 8. Capabilities of a Networked Collaborative Environment

interactions, allowing the utility of the information exchange to be significantly increased, helping to avoid information overload, improve timeliness, facilitate collaboration, and create the conditions for self-synchronization. These information-related capabilities are all enabled by the *post and smart pull* approach inherent to a robustly networked environment.

POST BEFORE PROCESSING

With the widespread adoption of IP (Internet Protocols), browser technology, and the creation of Web pages and portals, we can finally move away from a *push* approach to information dissemination to a *post and smart pull* approach. Moving from a *push* to a *post and smart pull* approach shifts the problem from the owner of information having to identify a large number of potentially interested parties to the problem of having the individual who needs information identifying potential sources of that information. The second problem is a far more tractable one. This is because it is much easier for the individual who has a need for information to determine its utility than for the producer to make this judgment.

Achieving this market-oriented vision will require continued investments in technologies such as improved browsers and information processing aids. It will also need to be supported by more robust data management tools and techniques. Continued advances in the area of data, such as XML, data warehousing, and data management policies that support the application of these technologies, are emerging quickly and appear very promising.[11]

To make this new information dissemination strategy work, organizations need to adopt a policy of *post before processing*. Such a policy serves to make certain that the network is populated with information in a timely way. Moreover, information originators will not necessarily stop with posting "raw" information. Many of them (for example, intelligence organizations, intermediate command centers, and entities outside of the DoD[12]) will also offer value-added services in which they put information into context, track information over time, and merge information with existing knowledge to produce richer products. These products will be posted so that they are available to users throughout the system.

To date, the result of these advances in information technology has been to both eliminate the requirement to be synchronous in time and space and to transform the problems associated with information dissemination from intractable ones to solvable ones.

LESSONS FROM THE PRIVATE SECTOR

Early proponents of an Information Age transformation in Defense are joined by counterparts in the private sector who also recognize that, in order to survive in the face of an uncertain and dynamic future, organizations need to develop new concepts of operation (business models), focus primarily on agility (rather than optimization), and apply *power to the edge* principles. Similar observations about the nature of the Information Age challenges faced and the nature of the solutions are shared by those studying financial markets, supply chains, credit cards, energy, and biotechnology. Some in industry also recognize the need to move from push-oriented to pull-oriented processes, but while we advocate this change in behavior for information dissemination, industry has applied this idea to supply chains. There is also a growing recognition in industry that they cannot, in the age of volatility, rely on one person's (a super star's) intuition to illuminate the path to the future.

A Focus on Agility

In the spring of 2003, Mankin and Chakrabarti[13] noted that the recent volatility in the financial markets was unprecedented (greater than at any time in the previous 70 years) and that, as is increasingly being articulated, the response to that volatility was agility (adaptability is one of its components). They hypothesized that successful companies would exhibit more adaptive behavior than less successful ones. They developed a set of markers (indicants) associated with adaptability that they hypothesized would be present in organizations that proved to be successful in periods of high volatility. They studied the performance of companies over 14 different industries in the closing decade of the 20th century, a period of relatively high volatility. They found that firms that had markers associated with adaptability significantly outperformed firms that did not. This result was even more convincing upon closer examination because firms that did not have markers associated with adaptability failed more often, and failed firms were excluded from the final tabulations. Agility (in this case, adaptability) did not just result in increased survival, but actually resulted in increased operating performance including sales growth, earnings growth, return on assets, and return on equity. Thus, agility seems to have outperformed optimization even on its home turf.[14]

Credit Cards to Biotechnology

Businesses are increasingly recognizing that they must become better able to respond to ever quickening changes in their environments and marketplaces.[15] As Johanna Woll said, this "means abandoning our management habits of prediction and control and developing instead the capacity to respond to change."[16] *Power to the edge* is the means to develop an increased capacity to respond to change. But how these principles are manifested will vary, as Woll points out, from enterprise to enterprise. At Capital One,[17] there was a recognition that interest rates and customer desires were changing faster than anyone in the credit card business was willing or able to respond to. Traditionally, decisions regarding who gets credit cards under what terms and conditions were always made by people exercising informed but subjective judgments. Capital One, in 1994, developed a computer-based approach involving data-mining. Using an empirically-based experimental approach, Capital One could then quickly target a variety of market segments and develop and field test customized credit products. This experimental approach (they called it "test and learn culture") has spread to other aspects of Capital One business including recruiting, hiring, and evaluating employee performance.

At British Petroleum (BP), Lord John Browne acknowledged that volatility had become the norm, not the exception, and sought to develop the capability to respond to volatility better than his competition. In fact, he aimed to make volatility his friend, not his enemy. A major part of his strategy was to move far more aggressively into the development of a full portfolio of products that were not expected to be significant for decades and to adopt a "green" approach to energy. BP has grown significantly (mergers and acquisitions) over the past few years into a global and diverse enterprise encompassing about 150 business units in 80 countries. Managing this much diversity while ensuring responsiveness to the dynamics of many markets requires a fundamental focus on agility. Lord Browne's approach was to summon his top management team to London and instill in them a set of behavioral rules that would (hopefully) result in desirable emergent behaviors.

In biotechnology, a focus on adaptation comes naturally. Instead of engineering their products, they breed populations of molecules, creating variability through bioengineering and selectively recombining the best performers. Hence the final product emerges. Agility is an inherent property of this accelerated process of evolution. This represents a radical departure from the traditional approach pharmaceutical companies used to develop drugs. This traditional method involved not only knowing the objective, but also how to achieve it.

At Maxygen, a biotech firm in Redwood City, California, evolution is not only how they approach product development, but it is also their business model. They refrained from setting out to capture a particular market or market segment, and rather let the market decide–an opportunity-based strategy they called "planned opportunism."

From Push to Pull-Oriented Supply Chain

A revolution is also taking place in agribusiness. The ability to respond is a function of awareness. Information flow is vital to the ability to create awareness and yet agribusiness has traditionally operated by trying to provide seeds and crop protection to farmers around the world without really knowing what these farmers want. This is because distributors are information sinks, inhibiting the flow of information between farmers and suppliers. The traditional supply chain model involves product push from suppliers to distributors, who handle customer interactions. A new business model is being explored, one that tries to create farmer pull by promoting products directly to farmers and may, in the future, involve direct Internet ordering. With a direct line to the farmer, suppliers are now better connected to farmers and can understand and act more quickly in response to changes in farmer attitudes and behavior.

This is becoming increasingly important because of the increasing complexity and volatility of the market. The advent of genetic engineering and the desire for integrated solutions (seeds plus protection) have resulted in a greater segmentation of the marketplace, an increased need for information to flow, and, because of changing consumer attitudes, the need to keep abreast of opinions and behaviors. Moving from an arms-length arrangement with farmers to a direct, information-rich connection, suppliers are creating the conditions necessary to become more agile.

A better understanding of the market is only the first step toward agility. A company also needs to be able to respond more quickly. Leading companies[18] in agribusiness are also moving from product development to offer development and to an adaptive supply chain.[19] Company scientists and product developers are spending less time in the lab and more time in the field talking to farmers to better understand their needs and work with them on integrated solutions. With this increased collaboration, products are better tailored. This increase in understanding and collaboration also provides the basis for developing niche products that have significant competitive advantages.

To complete the transformation, companies will need to abandon a made-for-stock or inventory mentality and replace it with an adaptive supply chain. Obviously this cannot be done without (1) the move to a pull-oriented supply chain and (2) the anticipation that results from collaboration. Currently, the key impediment to an adaptive supply chain is a long development process. Future increases in agility will be paced by their ability to move products through development more rapidly to the market.

Demise of the Super Star

In the organizational equivalent of natural selection, leaders in industry and senior commanders in the military have long been selected for their superior intuition. They see things that others do not see. Klein[20] has shown that experts, those we turn to for direction and guidance, use intuition rather than rational decisionmaking to make sense of situations. These experts discern patterns and relate these patterns to their prior experience and/or knowledge to determine the nature of the situation and the appropriate response. Human intuition and recognition-primed decisionmaking[21] were advanced[22] as the solution to the breakdown of Industrial Age approaches to decisionmaking.

It is becoming increasingly clear that the complexity of the situations faced and the responses needed have outpaced not only decision theoretic approaches, but have also outpaced the ability of even the best of experts (super stars) to deal with the complexities involved. First, the sources of complexity are accelerating. These sources of complexity include the variety of events and entities that are connected, the density of the interactions, and the speed of interactions that make it difficult to relate a cause to an effect and almost impossible to predict cascading effects. Second, it takes a long time for individuals to become experts and senior decisionmakers in industry and the military, spending decades to arrive in positions of leadership. This means that the bulk of their experience is well aged, increasingly out-of-date, and of questionable relevance. At some point, these individuals face situations that bear little resemblance to anything that they have previously experienced. These differences emerge as quantitative, but at some point these differences become qualitative in nature. Revolutions, whether they are in military affairs or in business affairs, involve changes in rule sets. Not only is the situation different and the patterns unfamiliar, but the very logic that relates problems and solutions changes as well. Bonabeau[23] makes many of these points and concludes that intuition is not only unlikely to help (in the face of growing complexity and volatility), but may often be misleading. Statisticians need to constantly remind analysts not to try to take regression analysis beyond the sampled range or population. Scientists warn about the dangers of making inferences.

Rather than rely on individual genius, Information Age processes tap collective knowledge and collaboration. Examples of the power and promise of such an approach already abound. In 2001, Microsoft launched a Web-based game to promote the Spielberg film "A.I." The content of the game was scattered across the entire Internet, and the challenges built into the game required knowledge of "everything from Photoshop to Greek mythology, 3D sculpting, molecular biology, computer coding, and lute tablature." The puzzles were meant to be so demanding that no individual could possibly complete them all. But immediately after the discovery of the game on the Web, teams of curious players developed organically across the country. Working together, their combined knowledge allowed them to complete the first 3 months' worth of game content in only 1 day.[24] These teams excelled at solving problems, and they could do so at surprising speeds.[25] However, learning the work processes associated with information sharing, exploiting collective knowledge, and conducting the efficient, authoritative collaboration will require establishing new mind sets (education and training) as well as new tools.

Without being able to fall back on traditional approaches to strategic planning, without being able to rely on intuition, from where does leadership and direction now come? The answer for industry is the same as for the military; constantly dealing with unfamiliar situations places a premium on agility in all of its dimensions. The approach to developing the agile organization that BP has adopted, like the Information Age approach to command and control presented in this book, is based on the application of *power to the edge* principles. This enables an enterprise to bring all of its available information and its brain power to bear by allowing information to be recombined in untold ways and by allowing individuals to interact in unplanned ways to create understandings and options not previously possible.

EFFICIENCY: HIERARCHIES V. THE ROBUSTLY NETWORKED FORCE

One of the misperceptions that has dogged discussions of Network Centric Warfare and *power to the edge* is the idea that a robustly networked force will be inefficient, demanding massive bandwidth and requiring large investments of time and effort by the users.

Figure 9 illustrates the first point. The simple Industrial Age hierarchy appears to have very few connections when compared with a fully connected Information Age system with the same number of nodes. Hence, naïve analysts conclude that the bandwidth requirements for a robustly networked force must, by definition, be massive and supportable only at enormous cost.

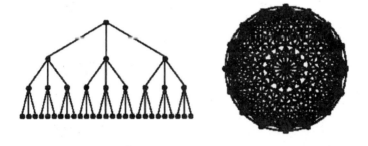

Figure 9. Hierarchical (left) and Fully Connected (right) Networks

In fact, however, richly networked systems, such as the Internet, are highly bandwidth-efficient because the actual number of interactions that take place is not the theoretically possible maximum, but is instead organized around communities of interest and is driven by circumstances.[26] In fact, many of the interactions that need to take place are more efficiently accomplished in a networked environment because middlemen are eliminated. The Internet, for example, has a small number of very richly employed nodes (Google, for example) that are used by many users, a secondary set of intermediate nodes that are functionally organized and used by those in particular communities, and a large number of nodes (the vast majority) that are connected to a modest subset of the network. This pattern is reflected in Figure 10 and is obviously much more efficient than what is implied in the fully connected alternative.

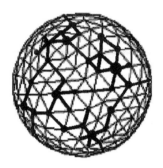

Figure 10. Power to the Edge—while all nodes are connected, only a small number emerge as bandwidth-intensive centers of activity

The alleged inefficiency of a robustly networked force in terms of time and effort required is also a myth. First, in a robust network, the burden of ensuring proper distribution is shifted toward the users of information, who must be empowered through training and tools to know what information is relevant to their situation, where they can find it, and how value-added services can be used to support them. Investments here in ensuring adequate interoperability and agility in the use of the system will be much more efficient than the continuous investment, time delays, misdistribution, and blocked channels resulting from efforts to maintain an Industrial Age hierarchical system that is based on predefined information requirements matrices. Secondly, while collaborative processes have been shown (in laboratory experiments with ad hoc groups) to slow decisionmaking (while improving its quality for complex decisions),[27] groups that have worked together over time and across situations prove to be much faster without having to sacrifice decision quality. Military organizations, of course, spend considerable time and energy in training and exercises precisely so they will be able to work together quickly and effectively. Hence, while collaborative processes make demands on doctrine, organization, training, and leadership, they actually are every bit as efficient (and under certain circumstances, more efficient) as noncollaborative processes. When the likelihood of better decisions is taken into account and the fact that better decisions avoid having to make decisions about corrective action, these processes may well be more efficient. (In the classic phrase, why is there never time to do it right, but always time to do it over?) Getting the job done right the first time is highly efficient.

NOTES

1 Madrick, Jeff. "The Business Media and the New Economy." Research Paper R-24. Boston, MA; Harvard University Press. 2001. p. 7. http://www.ksg.harvard.edu/presspol/publications/R-24Madrick.PDF. (Apr 1, 2003)

2 The chapter on the Information Age in *Network Centric Warfare* provides a succinct overview of the nature of the Information Age. A more comprehensive treatment can be found in the three-volume *Information Age Anthology*.
Alberts, *Network*. p. 15.
Alberts, *Information Age Anthology*.

3 See the discussion of What's Different: Alberts, *Understanding*. p. 44.

4 Toffler, Alvin. *The Third Wave*. New York, NY: Bantam Books. 1991.
Bacon, Sir Francis. *Meditationes Sacrae*. 1597.

5 Alberts, *Information Age Anthology, Volume 1*.

6 This discussion draws directly from a number of presentations given by the Honorable John Stenbit, the Assistant Secretary of Defense (Command, Control, Communications, and Intelligence).

7   These were adapted from a 2-dimensional view proposed by Evans and Wurster and first introduced in Alberts' *Understanding Information Age Warfare*, pages 95-102.

8   Note that at this time, data processing and storage as well as bandwidth were rather expensive.

9   Note that e-mail came about at a time when processing and storage costs had been significantly reduced, but while bandwidth was still relatively expensive.

10 The availability of a networked environment results from the change in the economics of information. At this point in time, processing, storage, and bandwidth are available at relatively low costs with expectations for even lower costs in the future.

11 Chief Information Officer, Department of Defense. "Data Management." House of Representatives Report 107-532. March 15, 2003.

12 Weblogs, also known as Blogs, have been around for a couple of years. Blogs are, in effect, individual postings of information (facts, opinion, analysis) by a wide variety of credible and less credible sources. More recently, passive social software has been developed to monitor, track, and analyze Blogs and links to and from Blogs (e.g. www.technorati.com)

13 Mankin, Eric, and Prabal Chakrabarti. "Valuing Adaptability: Markers for Managing Financial Volatility." *Perspectives on Business Innovation*. Issue 9. Cambridge, MA: Center for Business Innovation. Spring 2003. http://www.cbi.cgey.com/journal/issue9/not_all.htm. (Mar 31, 2003)

14 The agility argument is based upon giving up some performance in a hedge against uncertainty, thus one might expect a lower rate of return (as in savings accounts vs. stock) in return for lower risk.

15 Yam, Yaneer Bar. *Dynamics of Complex Systems*. New England Complex Systems Institute. Reading, MA: Addison-Wesley Publishing. 1997. http://necsi.org/publications/dcs/index.html (May 1, 2003)

16 Woll, Johanna. "Not All Adaptive Enterprises are Alike." *Perspectives on Business Innovation*. Issue 9. Cambridge, MA: Center for Business Innovation. Spring 2003. http://www.cbi.cgey.com/journal/issue9/not_all.htm. (Mar 31, 2003)

17 These stories about corporate attempts to be more responsive come from material developed by Meyer and Davis for their forthcoming book, *It's Alive: The Coming Convergence of Information, Biology, and Business*, and reported on in Woll's article, "Not All Adaptive Enterprises are Alike."

18 These companies are not named in Robert Gray's article, "Cultivating the Customer: Reaping the rewards of the Supply Chain."

19 Gray, Robert. "Cultivating the Customer: Reaping the rewards of the Supply Chain." *Perspectives on Business Innovation*. Issue 9. Cambridge, MA: Center for Business Innovation. Spring 2003. http://www.cbi.cgey.com/journal/issue9/not_all.htm. (Mar 31, 2003)

20 Klein, Gary. *Intuition at Work: Why Developing Your Gut Instincts Will Make You Better at What You Do*. New York, NY: Doubleday Publishing. December 2002.
Klein, Gary. *Sources of Power: How People Make Decisions*. Cambridge, MA: MIT Press. January 1998.

21 The act of identifying a stimulus.

22 Stewart, Thomas A. "Right from the Gut: Investing with Naturalistic Decision Making." *The Consilient Observer*. Vol 1, Issue 22. Dec 3, 2002.

23 Bonabeau, Eric. "When Intuition is Not Enough." *Perspectives on Business Innovation*. Issue 9. Cambridge, MA: Center for Business Innovation. Spring 2003.
http://www.cbi.cgey.com/journal/issue9/when_intuition.htm. (Mar 31, 2003)

24 Lee, Elan. "This is Not a Game: A Discussion of the Creation of the AI Web Experience." Presented at the 16th annual Game Developers Conference. March 19-23, 2002.

25 Herz, J.C. *Joystick Nation: How Videogames Ate Our Quarters, Won Our Hearts, and Rewired Our Minds*. New York, NY: Little, Brown & Company. 1997.

26 See Network Centric Warfare/Network Enabled Capabilities Workshop, 17-19 December 2002 on www.dodccrp.org.

27 Druzhinin, V.V. and D.S. Kontorov. "Concept, Algorithm, and Decision," Moscow, *Voinizdat*, 1972.
Nofi, Albert. "Defining and Measuring Shared Situational Awareness." Center for Naval Analyses DARPA, November 2000.
Schulz-Hardt, Stefan. "Productive conflict in group decision making: Genuine and contrived dissent as strategies to counteract biased information seeking." *Organizational Behavior and Human Decision Processes*. New York; Jul 2002; Vol. 88, Iss. 2; p. 563.
Artman, Henrik. "Situation awareness and co-operation within and between hierarchical units in dynamic decision making." *Ergonomics*. London; Nov 1999; Vol. 42, Iss. 11; p. 1404.

Chapter 6

Desired Characteristics of Information Age Forces

M uch has been written about the post-Cold War security environment, including the threats posed by nonstate actors armed with weapons of mass destruction and disruption, the implications of globalization, the Internet, and ubiquitous "news" coverage, as well as our vulnerabilities to information and critical infrastructure-related attacks.[1] It is clear that traditional military forces and capabilities alone are not adequate to meet these Information Age security challenges.

The shortcomings of existing force structure, concepts of operation, organization, doctrine, personnel, education, training, material, and systems can be identified by looking at the minimum essential capabilities required for successful military operations and assessing the ability of current forces to accomplish these tasks in the context of the 21st century security environment. Four minimum essential capabilities are required for a given operation:

1. The ability to make sense of the situation;

2. The ability to work in a coalition environment including nonmilitary (interagency, international organizations and private industry, as well as contractor personnel) partners;

3. Possession of the appropriate means to respond; and

4. The ability to orchestrate the means to respond in a timely manner.

Three of these four essential capabilities involve command and control. The third is about the tools of war and policy implementation. This book, with its focus on the transformation of command and control, thus addresses changes in the way we think about information and relationships.

NETWORK CENTRIC WARFARE

Network Centric Warfare provides the theory for warfare in the Information Age. It is, as the NCW Report to Congress stated, "no less than the embodiment of an Information Age transformation of the DoD."[2] As such we can look to its tenets to see what is different about the information assumed to be available, how it is distributed and used, and how individuals and entities relate to one another. In other words, we can identify what is different about command and control.

The tenets of Network Centric Warfare[3] serve to provide the basis for a value chain stretching from a set of specific force capabilities to operational effectiveness and agility. Such a value chain can provide a context for assessing both the value of changes in a measure or set of measures, as well as a context for determining the validity of the NCW tenets themselves. Recent work[4] has resulted in the development of an NCW Conceptual Framework (Figure 11) that employs the tenets of NCW as its point of departure.[5] This framework encompasses the four aforementioned capabilities and identifies in detail the characteristics and attributes needed by Information Age forces, their relationships to one another, and measures of the extent that these characteristics and attributes are realized.

Figure 11 focuses on the C2-related capabilities that are integral to Information Age forces. It is important to note that this framework not only includes variables related to individual sensemaking and decisionmaking,[6] but mirrors this set of variables with a set of variables that pertain to team, group, or organizational sensemaking and decisionmaking capabilities. These team, group, and organizational attributes include the degree to which (1) information is shared and (2) shared awareness is achieved. These variables are at the heart of the collaborative processes and self-synchronizing behaviors that NCW seeks to exploit.

The logic of the NCW value chain begins with the characteristics of force entities. These include effectors (all those able to create effects, not just weapons), information sources, value-added services, and of course, command and control entities. Individual entities have access to organic capabilities including organic information sources. The degree to which force entities are networked will determine the quality of information

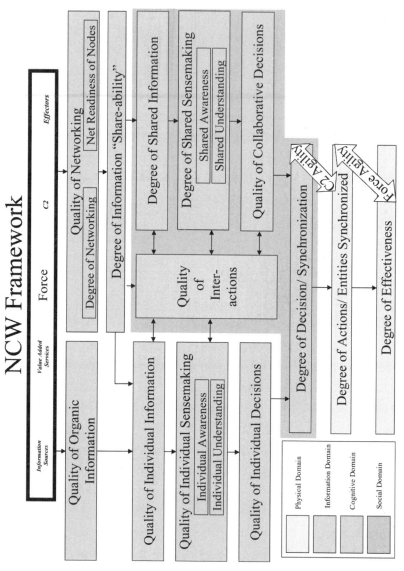

Figure 11. Network Centric Warfare Conceptual Framework

that is available to various force entities and their ability to interact in the information domain. The level of interoperability achieved and the characteristics of command and control processes will determine the extent that information is shared, as well as the nature and quality of the interactions that occur between and among force entities. Taken together, these capabilities and organizational characteristics will determine the effectiveness of the force, its agility, and the degree to which decisions, plans, actions, and entities are synchronized.

SENSEMAKING

Making sense of a situation begins with putting the available information about the situation into context and identifying the relevant patterns that exist. Developing situation awareness[7] has always been a challenge in war. A great deal of money has been invested over the years in ISR (Intelligence, Surveillance, and Reconnaissance) assets and the systems that collect, process, and carry this information. ISR is an effort to minimize the "fog of war."[8] The capability now exists to detect, identify, track, and destroy (at stand-off distances) traditional military formations of tanks, ships at sea, and aircraft in flight. This capability has forced adversaries to adapt in a variety of ways (e.g., cover, concealment, and deception) as seen in Bosnia and Kosovo.[9] Of course, Information Age adversaries will not necessarily employ traditional military platforms and hence will not be as easily detected, identified, or tracked. Being able to pick a nontraditional adversary out of the noise and determine its capabilities and intentions is among the greatest challenges that we face in the Information Age. The early experience in Iraq has underscored the importance of assessing both capabilities and will.

Being able to bring available information to bear involves more than collecting needed information. It also means being able to make information available to everyone who needs it, in a form that they can use it, in a secure and timely manner. Turning pieces of information into situation awareness requires the expertise and experience of many. Therefore, processes that bring available expertise and experience to bear and systems that support these processes are needed. This implies that a 21st century force needs to be robustly networked with information management capabilities that enable widespread information sharing and support simultaneous collaborations.

Sensemaking is much more than sharing information and identifying patterns. It goes beyond what is happening and what may happen to what can be done about it. This involves generating options, predicting adversary actions and reactions, and understanding the effect of particular courses of action (e.g., destroying a given target, initiating an attack on an enemy's flank). In the context of traditional military operations, the effects of destroying a target are not a particularly difficult problem because attrition of enemy capability is closely associated with the objectives of traditional military operations. In more recent military operations, with more restrictive rules of engagement (ROE), and with other than strictly military objectives, understanding the effects of such actions in their social, political, and economic contexts becomes critical. This is currently not a core competency. The need to be able to understand the direct and indirect effects of actions has increasingly been recognized. A recent book, *Effects Based Operations*,[10] explains the relationship between EBO and NCW and argues for explicit mapping of the effects of actions to objectives. The points made here have been driven home in operations in Bosnia, Kosovo, Afghanistan, and Iraq.

COALITION AND INTERAGENCY OPERATIONS

Few 21st century military operations will be unilateral. Perhaps one of the biggest challenges is forging and maintaining a coalition (of the willing or the politically necessary), a coalition that will in all likelihood include nonmilitary and/or nonstate actors. Interagency "coalitions" are of increasing importance, both at home and abroad. This complicates operations in a number of ways. For example, the effects of actions on coalition cohesion need to be added to the effects-based calculus.[11] In addition, effective coalition operations require that the members of the coalition achieve sufficient levels of interoperability in order to exchange information, to collaborate on command and control, and to achieve synchronous effects. This is a significant challenge.

APPROPRIATE MEANS

Traditional military means have primarily involved lethal force applied on the field of battle. Militaries have developed (and will continue to develop) nonlethal alternatives, including information weapons, and have developed peacekeeping, peace-enforcement, peacemaking, and nation building skills and capabilities. As operations in Iraq have demonstrated, the nature of emerging threats blurs the line between crime and war, as well as the boundaries of the battlefield. The battlefield is no longer confined to a contiguous area, nor does it have only a physical dimension. Cyberspace, with its lack of borders and sanctuaries, with its speed of light weapons, and its ability to cloak adversaries in anonymity, serves as the epitome of the 21st century battlespace. This, of course, has significant implications for what information is needed as well as who needs to be brought into a conversation about assessing a situation or what action is appropriate.

ORCHESTRATION OF MEANS

As has always been the case, the ability to act in concert in a timely manner often separates the victor from the vanquished. Acting in concert has, in the past, meant the ability to marshal or mass forces. In the Information Age, this meaning has changed to the massing of effects, often with widely dispersed forces and including nonkinetic means. *Timeliness*[12] is related to the situation at hand and hence is not the same as a *speedy* response. Rather, it is a response at the appropriate time. Nevertheless, the capability to act both collectively and quickly is important since it increases the likelihood that one will be able to act at the appropriate time. The time required is the sum of the time needed to make sense of the situation, decide what to do (or empower others to make these decisions), position forces, and act. While the physics of the means is a factor in this equation (including the time required to maneuver into position and deliver munitions), command and control is also always on the critical path. A significant part of this time budget has always been devoted to the processes and actions needed to synchronize forces and actions.

Synchronization, in a military context, is defined in Joint Publication 1-02 as "the arrangement of military actions in time, space, and purpose to produce maximum relative combat power at a decisive place and time."[13] Deliberate Planning[14] is currently the accepted military process to achieve force synchronization.

As the size of the force and/or the complexity of the operation increases, more and more of the time budget is devoted to achieving synchronization. Thus, the ability to act in a synchronized fashion and the ability to act quickly have been in tension. Not only is C2 a driving factor in the ability to respond in a timely manner, but it is, in fact, the major factor in the ability to achieve three out of the four minimum essential capabilities identified above. Thus, transforming C2 and related C4ISR capabilities to meet Information Age challenges is central to achieving an Information Age military. Furthermore, C2 characteristics are a major determinant in achieving agility. NCW, with its emphasis on shared sense-making and self-synchronization, aims to allow forces to be simultaneously better synchronized and quicker. *Power to the edge* is the principle that needs to be adopted to achieve this.

In order for a force to possess the capabilities described above, the force needs, in addition to specific mission and task-related capabilities, two key force-level attributes: *interoperability* and *agility*. These are discussed in the following two chapters.

NOTES

1   Friedman, Thomas. *The Lexus and the Olive Tree*. New York, NY: Anchor Books. 2000.
    Kwak, Chris, and Robert Fagin. *Internet 3.0. Equity Research Technology*. Bear Stearns. 2001.
    https://access.bearstearns.com/supplychain/infrastructure.pdf (Feb 1, 2003)

2   This is the first sentence of the Executive Summary of: *Network Centric Warfare Department of Defense Report to Congress*. July 2001.

3   Alberts, *Network*.

4   *Network Centric Warfare Conceptual Framework*. Network Centric Warfare and Network Enabled Capabilities Workshop: Overview of Major Findings. Dec 17-19, 2002. OSD(NII) in conjunction with RAND and EBR, Inc.

5   Department of Defense, Office of the Assistant Secretary of Defense for Command, Control, Communications, and Intelligence (OASD/NII), Command and Control Research Program (CCRP). http://www.dodccrp.org/ncw_workshop/NCWDecWork.htm. (Apr 1, 2003)

6   Sensemaking encompasses the range of cognitive activities undertaken by individuals, teams, organizations, and indeed societies to develop awareness and understanding and to relate this understanding to a feasible action space.
Alberts, *Information Age Transformation*. pp. 136-7.

7   When the term *situation awareness* is used, it describes the awareness of a situation that exists in part or all of the battlespace at a particular point in time. Awareness occurs in the cognitive domain, in people's heads, not within the information systems that support people.
Alberts, *Understanding*. p. 120.

8   Clausewitz, Carl von. Michael E. Howard and Peter Paret, eds. *On War*. Princeton, NJ: Princeton University Press. 1976. p. 101.

9   Wentz, *Bosnia*.
Wentz, *Kosovo*.

10   Smith, *Effects*.

11   Smith, *Effects*. p. 336.

12   Timeliness is another factor that depends on the situation. It reflects the relationship between the age of an information item and the tasks or missions it must support. Alberts, *Understanding*. p85.

13   Department of Defense Dictionary of Military and Associated Terms. Joint Pubs 1-02. p. 424.

14   Deliberate Planning is defined as: The Joint Operation Planning and Execution System process involving the development of joint operation plans for contingencies identified in joint strategic planning documents. Deliberate planning is accomplished in prescribed cycles that complement other Department of Defense planning cycles in accordance with the formally established Joint Strategic Planning System. DoD Dictionary of Military and Associated Terms.
http://www.dtic.mil/doctrine/jel/doddict/data/d/01562.html (Feb 1, 2003)

Chapter 7

Interoperability

This chapter discusses the need for interoperability in future military operations, what is required to achieve interoperability, the characteristics of various approaches to interoperability, the nature of the challenges involved, and how a *power to the edge* approach makes interoperability more attainable.

NEED FOR INTEROPERABILITY

The basic tenets of NCW (Figure 12) begin with the existence of a robustly networked force. Such a force can only be achieved if there is a high level of interoperability among mission participants and the systems that support them.

Interoperability, the ability to work together, needs to simultaneously occur at a number of levels or layers[1] to enable entities to communicate, share information, and collaborate with

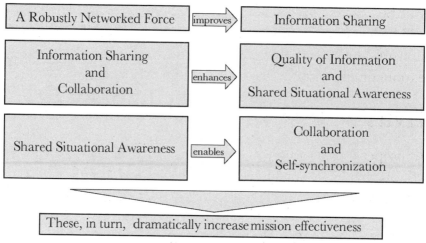

Figure 12. The Tenets of NCW

one another. The degree to which forces are interoperable directly affects their ability to conduct network-centric operations. Interoperability must be present in each of the four domains: physical, information, cognitive, and social. First, all force entities, as well as the other entities that the force needs to work with, need to be connected to the net.[2] Second, they need to be able to provide information to those on the net. Third, they need to be able to find, retrieve, and understand the information available on the net. Fourth, they may need to participate in one or more virtual collaboration environments or processes. A lack of connectivity or interoperability on the part of an entity, or subset of entities, makes it difficult for them to contribute to the mission. Entities that are not interoperable or have limited interoperability will not have access to all available information, will not be able to provide information to entities that may need it, and will be limited in the ways that they can collaborate and work together with others. As a result, their value (ability to contribute to combat power or mission effectiveness) will be limited over time. These entities will be marginalized. As a result, the value of the enterprise will be less than it could have been. This conclusion is a reflection of Metcalf's Law that the value of a network increases exponentially with the number of nodes (participants).[3]

LEVELS OF INTEROPERABILITY

Interoperability can be understood as a spectrum of connectedness that ranges from unconnected, isolated entities to fully interactive, sharing enterprises.

There are varying degrees of interoperability, of course. The levels of network-centric capability defined in the NCW maturity model[4] (depicted below) directly correspond to the degree to which interoperability has been achieved.

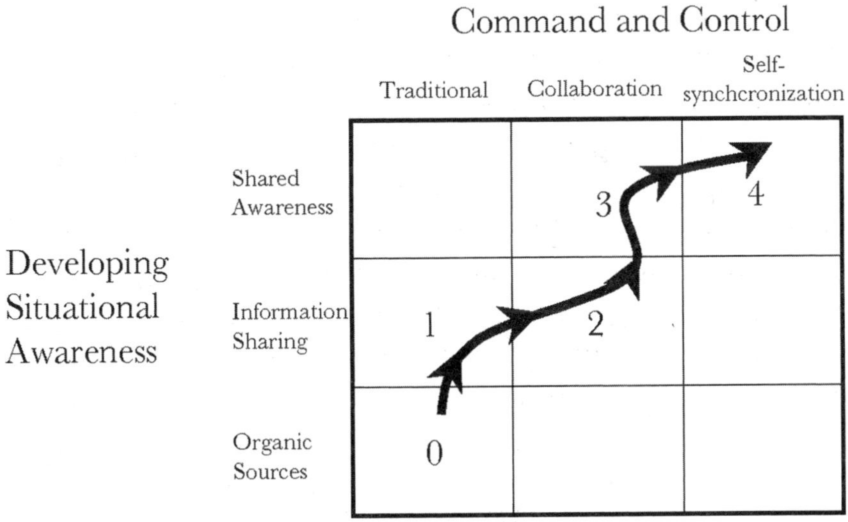

Figure 13. NCW Maturity Model[5]

Level 0 requires limited interoperability and information sharing. The interoperability that exists is based upon IERs (Information Exchange Requirements) developed from existing organizations, processes, and systems. Level 1 requires that more entities are able to share information. Level 2 requires sufficient interoperability for entities to participate in collaborative environments and processes. Level 3 requires that entities be interoperable not only in the information domain, but also in the cognitive domain, so that shared awareness can be achieved. Level 4 requires interoperability in the social domain so that actions can be dynamically self-synchronized. Thus, moving up from one level to another requires more interoperability in all three of the dimensions of the information domain (richness, reach, and quality of interactions) as well as interoperability in more domains (not only the information domain but also the cognitive and social domains). Technology is crucial, but is inadequate without appropriate adaptations in organizations, work processes, and attitudes.

The quest for interoperability is not new, but it has never been so important. While advances in technology, the proliferation of computers and communications capabilities, and the rise of e-business have made it easier than ever to achieve widespread interoperability, several major obstacles to progress remain. The challenges and how they may be addressed are discussed later. First, it is important to understand what is needed to enable two or more entities to be interoperable.

ACHIEVING INTEROPERABILITY

Achieving interoperability involves a lot of sheer effort and the application of knowledge from many different disciplines in each of the four key domains. Yet, individuals working in a particular organization or domain are often unaware of the challenges that need to be faced in other areas of that domain or other domains. Despite this, all of their perspectives and work, within and across organizations or domains, need to come together to achieve the level of interoperability that enables network-centric operations at the highest levels of NCW maturity.[6]

To illustrate this point, consider the nature of telephone interactions. What is required in each of the domains to achieve functional interoperability? Telephone calls are so commonplace that few people think about what it takes to make them possible and what makes them useful. To begin with, there is a lot that needs to happen to make it possible for one person to pick up a phone and talk to someone else virtually anywhere. Whether one or more of the parties is stationary or mobile, whether the parties are in the same country or even on the same continent, whether they are in the air, on the water, or in space, all telephone calls require certain elements. For a telephone conversation to take place, physical signals must be exchanged over a circuit[7] established between the two telephone sets or devices. First of course, a person's voice needs to be converted by the device into a signal that can be transmitted over large distances. Then these signals travel as electrical impulses over wires (twisted pair or coaxial cables), as light waves in fiber, as radio signals in the air, as focused laser beams, or some combination of the above. As is the case in many telephone calls, these signals need to transverse from one medium into another.[8] The physical domain contains the devices, media, and connectors that provide the pathways that transform signals from one medium to another and transport signals from place to place. Embedded in the signals are address-related information and content. If the path of the signal involves more than one medium, then a signal conversion needs to take place. If and when the signal reaches a branching point or a switch, then the address-related information (or a part of it) needs to be understood so that the signal is sent to the right place. Thus, in addition to being interoperable in the physical domain, interoperability needs to be achieved in the information domain to ensure that a signal gets to its intended destination and that the content remains intact. With the content intact at the intended destination, all that remains is for the device at the destination to transform the signal into audible sound with sufficient fidelity to be properly perceived. This can involve interoperability in both the physical and information domains. The transformations that take place include transitions between analogue and digital information representations, and between these information representations and audible manifestations. Interoperability also needs to be achieved in the cognitive domain to ensure that the sounds transmitted from one ear to another are not babble but make sense to the receiver.[9] Finally, the exchange of information or the collaboration that takes place during a phone conversation requires some degree of interoperability in the social domain. People must be able and willing to create a shared understanding of what has been said.

Figure 14 depicts the interoperability needed within and across domains to enable a useful verbal exchange between two individuals.[10]

Approaches to Interoperability

Two entities can be interoperable (in, between, and among domains) if one of the following is true (Figure 15):

1. They both are capable of speaking in a common language (or protocol);

Physical Domain
where strike, protect, and maneuver take place across different environments

Information Domain
where information is created, manipulated, and shared

Cognitive Domain
where perceptions, awareness, beliefs, and values reside and where, as a result of sensemaking, decisions are made

Social Domain
set of interactions between and among force entities

Figure 14. The Domains of Warfare

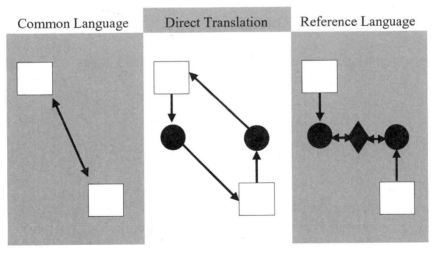

Common Language   Direct Translation   Reference Language

Figure 15. Multiple Language Interactions

2. They have a direct two-way translator that can translate one party's language into the other's; or

3. There exists a common reference language and each of the parties has a translator to translate their language into the reference language.

These alternative approaches differ in their practicality, scalability, and the burdens that they place on organizations and entities.

An example of a common language approach to interoperability in the information domain is the use of English as the lingua franca of air traffic control. This approach is practical in this case because air traffic control is a highly regulated, relatively small, and specialized community (and as an invitation-only international fraternity it can set and enforce standards). For the most part, a common language approach works under these conditions, even when participants have a very diverse set of native languages. There have been incidents of communications breakdowns, with disastrous consequences, but those breakdowns are very rare.

If standards can be enforced, then this approach scales well. That is, new members to the conversation only need to master one language, English (and the specialized terminology), while current members need to do nothing as the population grows. As long as English is adequate for the purposes of air traffic control, this approach will work.

But what if participants refuse to agree on a common language? For example, in NATO there are two official languages (English and French). This complicates things a bit, but having just a few acknowledged options also scales well. In this case, each participant needs to choose one of two languages in which to be fluent and needs to do nothing as new members enter the organization. However, there is now a need for simultaneous translation and NATO meetings require bilingual translators. To work, both the languages and the translators need to keep up to date with new concepts (and objects) to be complete and accurate. When they fail to keep abreast of new words or phrases, their ability to convey appropriate meanings will degrade. Thus, any approach involving translation requires simultaneous maintenance of the languages and the translator(s). Therefore, agreeing on two common languages is almost as good as agreeing on one and may be much more attractive to potential participants. When translation can be accomplished fully automatically and with great accuracy, then the number of standard languages that can be tolerated will increase somewhat.

But what happens when such an agreement cannot be reached and each participant insists on speaking their own language? Unless the parties can agree on a reference language, the interoperability problem takes a sharp turn for the worse. Instead of scaling at a linear rate as new entities join the conversation, the burden increases exponentially as new members are added.

Take the worst case scenario: each of the entities insists on using their own unique language. With no agreement on standard languages or a reference language, two-way translators need to proliferate with the square of the number of unique languages (Figure 16). When a new participant with a unique language joins a group with n different languages (protocols or formats), the joiner must come with n two-way translators in order to be able to receive signals or information from current participants. In addition, and perhaps more importantly, each of the *n* current participants must install a translator. As *n* increases from a small number to a large number, this burden quickly becomes unsustainable.

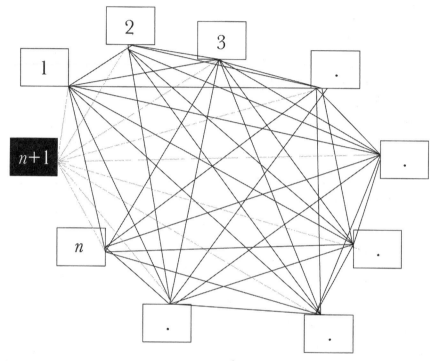

Figure 16. An n^2 Problem[11]

Thus, minimizing the difficulty and cost of achieving the level of interoperability necessary to conduct network-centric operations depends upon our ability to avoid having to rely on an "n^2" approach.

Interoperability Challenges

Previous efforts to achieve interoperability among force entities have been frustrated, despite the visible need for interoperability. This need has been forcibly brought to public attention by virtue of a number of high profile operational failures. Efforts at achieving interoperability have, in the past, been frustrated because of a combination of formidable obstacles. The result is a legacy of largely noninteroperable entities and the use of retrofitted translators on a case-by-case basis. This makes it tedious and costly to facilitate information exchanges. The result has been to focus on those information exchanges that seem important based upon existing organizational arrangements and the way we do business today (current work processes and procedures).

This emphasis on the identification of Information Exchange Requirements that can be used to set priorities for investing in interoperability and in specifying requirements for systems is most unfortunate. For one thing, it detracts attention from the fact that information needs to be *widely* shared, not just shared with whoever information is currently shared with or additional entities that can be identified in advance. Legacy mindsets about the need for and nature of jointness (that it applies only to the operational level) have resulted in a lack of appreciation of the need for peer-to-peer interoperability at the tactical level. This blind spot causes those who draft requirements to draft them far too narrowly. To a large extent, it is a chicken and egg situation, with the recognition of a need to exchange information being dependent on being interoperable so that this need may be discovered.

Even if it were possible to correctly and completely identify IERs for a given entity, information sharing needs change as new entities and new capabilities are deployed and as a function of mission and environment, both of which are changing in ways that cannot be fully anticipated. Hence, it is important to realize that the need for interoperability is a basic one, not an appliqué that can be added on for specific IERs. Thus, the IER approach to interoperability is leading us down a path that makes it more and more difficult to achieve interoperability with each passing year. From a transformation perspective, this makes it difficult to support the widespread information sharing needed for network-centric operations. The result is that new concepts of operation and operations with coalitions of the willing (including interagency and international organizations of all types) are disadvantaged.

We need to adopt a more effective approach to interoperability. Any such approach needs to effectively deal with the current obstacles. Major obstacles include not only a significant amount of noninteroperable legacy capability, but continual advances in technology and a program-centric approach to acquisition. This book is about moving power to the edge, an Information Age approach to both organizations and architectures. This approach will enable organizations to make the most of the information that is available.

AN EDGE APPROACH TO INTEROPERABILITY

An approach to interoperability with *power to the edge* characteristics promises to make interoperability a more tractable problem because the move to a *post and smart pull* approach frees us from the tyranny of IERs. Posting using IP frees information sources from the requirement to package their information in *n-1* ways. Consumers of information (which also includes most information sources and producers) need only to be Web-enabled to pull information. Understanding the information will require the addition of semantic interoperability and a degree of shared expertise and experience.

Hence, assuming the worst case, only n changes need to be made to make the n systems Web-capable (not $n[n-1]/2$). Furthermore, as systems proliferate the burden goes up arithmetically, not exponentially. This is, in effect, a move away from application-to-application interoperability to *data* interoperability.

Some are bound to wonder whether or not a move to data interoperability represents progress rather than simply trading one impossible problem for another. After all, experience shows that the search for data standards has more often than not ended in frustration and failure. However, these failed efforts have tried to impose the same data definitions on disparate users. Data interoperability does not require everyone to adhere to the same standard. For example, the data element "date" can be represented in numerous ways (e.g., January 10, 2003, 01/10/03, 10/01/03, 01/10/2003, 10Jan2003, 20030110). All of these representations refer to the same date. Despite the fact that information sources could post date information in any one (or more) of these ways, interoperability can be achieved if the user of the information is aware of the different representations and their mapping to each other. The burden for this is shared between posters and pullers. If posters wish for their information to have value, then they need either to post the data in a widely recognized form or post it with metadata that provides the mapping to a recognized standard. If pullers wish to utilize available data, then they need to educate themselves regarding the various forms of the data element used by sources that they consider potentially valuable.

As the practice of *post and smart pull* is implemented, both information suppliers and consumers will become smarter. As a result, implementing a data-standards approach to systems interoperability among a collection of disparate and heterogeneous systems will be facilitated. Thus, the move from *smart push* to *post and smart pull* not only solves previously intractable problems by identifying important information and getting it to the right persons, but also facilitates the creation of the interoperability necessary to bring all relevant information and all relevant assets to bear. *Power to the edge* is therefore an inherently joint and coalition concept. It should be noted that without jointness (at all levels), shared situation awareness cannot be achieved. Shared situation awareness includes a shared understanding of command intent.

NOTES

1   There are several models that identify different layers, including the ISO model.
Blanchard, Eugene. *Introduction to Networking and Data Communications.* Southern Alberta Institute of Technology. 2000. Chapter 27.

2   The term *net* is used here to denote the collection of systems that constitute the DoD's GIG or global information grid. Department of Defense, Global Information Grid.
http://www.c3i.osd.mil/org/cio/doc/GPM11-8450.pdf. (March 27, 2003)

3   Metcalf's Law observes that although the cost of deploying a network increases linearly with the number of nodes in the network, the *potential* value of a network increases (scales) as a function of the square of the number of nodes that are connected by the network.
Alberts, *Network*. p. 250.

4   The NCW Maturity Model introduced in *Understanding Information Age Warfare* and included in the NCW Report to the Congress, relates the ability to achieve shared awareness and the nature of command and control to the ability to conduct network-centric operations.
Network Centric Warfare Department of Defense Report to Congress. July 2001.
Alberts, *Understanding.*

5   This depiction of the NCW Maturity Model replaces "Collaborative Planning" with "Collaboration" because in the future, planning and execution will merge.

6   Lest the reader think that the pursuit of interoperability is being undertaken solely to achieve a capability for NCW, it needs to be pointed out that in the 21st century security environment, widespread information sharing is needed to make sense of the situations that will occur regardless of how we choose to respond.

7   Physical or logical.

8   This is sometimes referred to as the transport layer.

9   This may require both a common language (e.g., English) and a mutual understanding of specific terms (e.g., military vocabulary or acronyms) plus some shared expertise and experience.

10 *Network Centric Warfare Conceptual Framework*, 2002.

11 Technically, it is really an $n(n-1)/2$ problem but for a sufficiently large n this reduces to an n squared problem. For further illustration, see: http://people.deas.harvard.edu/~jones/cscie129/lectures/lecture10/images/p_to_p.html. (June 1, 2003)

Chapter 8

Agility

INTRODUCTION

Agility is arguably one of the most important characteristics of successful Information Age organizations. Agile organizations do not just happen. They are the result of an organizational structure, command and control approach, concepts of operation, supporting systems, and personnel that have a synergistic mix of the right characteristics. The term *agile* can be used to describe each component of an organization's mission capability packages (MCPs), and/or an organization that can instantiate many MCPs. A lack of agility in one or more of these components will affect the overall agility of an organization. Thus, agile C2 can make much more of a positive difference in the context of an agile force than it would without such a force. However, without an operational concept that takes advantage of agile C2, the agility of a C2 system (human and equipment) will have only modest benefits. Similarly, an agile force that does not have an agile C2 system and operating concepts cannot perform close to its capacity.

Agile forces, MCPs, C2 systems, and operating concepts make sense regardless of the threat or the technology environment. However, the more uncertain and dynamic an adversary and/ or the environment are, the more valuable agility becomes. Since agility is a property that is manifested over a space (a range of values, a family of scenarios, a spectrum of missions) rather than being associated with a point in a space (a specific circumstance, a particular scenario, a given mission), agility represents capabilities that can be termed *scenario independent*. While we need scenario independence, traditional military planning is threat-based and relies on a few likely or most threatening scenarios. Threat-based planning (force structure investment based upon perceptions of capabilities of likely forces) arose because the greatest threat to most countries lay in one or a few hostile neighbors (for example, France and Germany in the 19th and early 20th centuries or Iran and Iraq in the 1980s) or in threats to the lines of communications between their home country and their colonies during the Age of Imperialism. The key to designing agile C2 is representing the diversity of threats and operating environments in a way that samples the future intelligently.

By identifying likely adversaries and the nature of their forces, military establishments could study their likely foes and design specific forces, operational concepts, and C2 systems to counteract them. Arms races then became quantitative as advantage was to be gained by numerical strength. For example, the treaties governing naval forces between the World

Wars assumed that there were "best" types of platforms (battleships, heavy and light cruisers, and aircraft carriers) that were available to all military establishments and could serve to counteract one another. Even the qualitative elements of such arms races (longer range guns, faster rates of fire, etc.) had a quantitative basis.

AGILITY: DEFINED AND PLACED IN AN INFORMATION AGE CONTEXT

The term *nimble* is sometimes used as a synonym for agile. It conjures up the correct image–the ability to move rapidly, but sure-footedly. Note that effectiveness (mission accomplishment) is an implicit assumption. As such, effectiveness is measured on a separate dimension from agility. Similarly, speed is not an end in itself, but a means to an end. Speed can make a response more effective or even make it possible for an organization to respond at all. But speed only enables effectiveness; it does not guarantee it. Hence, moving quickly, but not intelligently (in ways that improve the likelihood of success) would not, by our definition, constitute agility.

For example, had the U.S. and its Allies engaged the Iraqis in Kuwait as soon as they had forces on the ground in OPERATION DESERT STORM (Gulf War I), the battle would have been very different and friendly casualty rates may have been much higher. It is a question of the *need* to engage at a given point in time being properly meshed with the *ability* to engage at that point in time. Choosing instead to control the pace of that campaign and dictate the time, place, and form of the decisive engagements within it yielded a much better outcome than could have been obtained by attacking as soon as reasonably possible. Just as a mountain goat's agility involves the choice of when to leap and which rocks to land on, so too the agility of a military organization begins with its decisions about when, where, and how to engage. Indeed, as the classic observation by Sun Tzu states, "to win one hundred victories in one hundred battles is not the acme of skill. To subdue the enemy without fighting is the acme of skill."[1] In other words, a combination of agile maneuver and demonstrated military capability can prove sufficient for mission accomplishment without the need for forces to engage.

Industrial Age organizations are optimized for specific tasks or missions under specific assumptions about the operating environment, including the threat. They have problems, therefore, when confronted with rapid change (dynamics that carry their operating environments into unforeseen circumstances with no time to adjust) or great uncertainty (where the ideal organizational forms, work processes, and doctrines are not knowable). The problems the Germans experienced during World War II in combating partisans, the difficulties the colonial powers experienced during the Wars of National Liberation, and the U.S. experience in Vietnam are all examples of a lack of requisite agility in professional forces optimized for traditional, symmetric combat[2] with other professional militaries. Indeed, our very existence as a nation stems, at least in part, from the inability of British regulars to engage a different kind of army on a different kind of battlefield.

Agility is increasingly becoming recognized as the most critical characteristic of a transformed force, with network-centricity being understood as the key to achieving agility. Allies, most particularly the United Kingdom, are in the process of making agility a key feature of their forces and a fundamental objective of their C2 approaches. Agility cannot be considered to be merely an *attribute* of the C2 system; military establishments have recognized that agility considerations must *permeate* the mission capability package, operational concept, or force. This implies that the capability to be agile involves having not only the right material (e.g., sensors, infostructure, combat systems) but also the right doctrine, organization, personnel, training, and leadership. Moreover, it implies a need to coevolve these MCP elements through experimentation campaigns that assess not only mission effectiveness, but also agility. Indeed, coalition partners are concerned that they need to make the proper near-term investment decisions in order to keep pace with the U.S. transformation. While the specifics of the investments appropriate for any given country will differ as a function of the role(s) they wish to play and their existing legacy, they all would be well served if they focused on the degree to which their investment choices considered agility (and the ability to be network-centric as vital to achieving agility).

The potential for agility is greatly enhanced by the shared awareness and collaboration in Network Centric Warfare. In essence, richer information, cognitive, and social domains enable greater agility.

AGILE C2

This discussion focuses on agile C2, bearing in mind that agile C2 only makes sense in the context of agile forces and operational concepts. Agile individuals (commanders for example may differ in agility), organizations, C2 systems (personnel plus their supporting information systems and decision aids), and forces have a synergistic combination of the following six attributes, the key dimensions of agility:

1. Robustness: the ability to maintain effectiveness across a range of tasks, situations, and conditions;

2. Resilience: the ability to recover from or adjust to misfortune, damage, or a destabilizing perturbation in the environment;

3. Responsiveness: the ability to react to a change in the environment in a timely manner;

4. Flexibility: the ability to employ multiple ways to succeed and the capacity to move seamlessly between them;

5. Innovation: the ability to do new things and the ability to do old things in new ways; and

6. Adaptation: the ability to change work processes and the ability to change the organization.

While these attributes of agility are analytically distinct and often must be measured in different domains and contexts, in practice they are often interdependent. Moreover, when one of these attributes is lacking, the others are much more difficult to achieve. When they are all present, however, the likelihood of success (mission accomplishment) increases greatly. Each of these attributes is defined and discussed below.

Robustness

Robustness is the ability to retain a level of effectiveness across a range of missions that span the spectrum of conflict, operating environments, and/or circumstances. Robustness is often the first casualty when (1) operational concepts, (2) C2 systems, and (3) military forces are optimized against par-

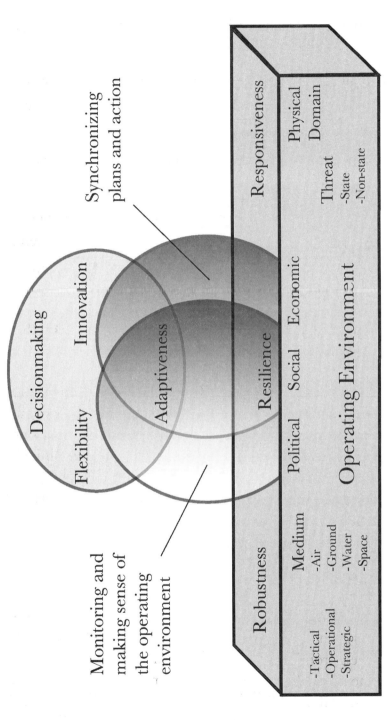

Figure 17. The Six Aspects of Agility in the Domains of Warfare

ticular threats. A major reason for their lack of robustness is the Industrial Age assumption that conflicts with less professional forces or operations that do not involve combat are "lesser included cases" that top of the line military organizations can deal with effectively.

As long as adversaries could be enticed into the open or forced to defend specific locations (e.g., behave symmetrically, like professional militaries), the superior training, firepower, and maneuverability of professional military organizations would allow them to accomplish missions. Hence, counterguerilla operations, from Indian campaigns in the United States to efforts by the French in Indochina, sought to create strong points that could be defended against attack and to launch attacks against locations the guerrillas had to defend. These were means of forcing traditional combat on nontraditional forces.

However, as learned by the French in Spain during the Napoleonic Wars, the British in the Boer War, the Turks in North Africa and Arabia during World War I, the Germans in Europe during World War II, the Japanese in the Philippines during World War I, and the U.S. in Vietnam, well organized and highly motivated irregular forces that can refuse combat under unfavorable conditions are exceptionally difficult to defeat with forces that are optimized for traditional combat.

The Industrial Age military's lack of robustness comes into sharp focus because the range of military missions that must be supported has expanded. Peace operations of various sorts (peacemaking, peace-enforcement, peacekeeping, etc.) and humanitarian assistance efforts,[3] as well as very complex and ambiguous missions, have become commonplace. U.S. missions in Haiti moved in a matter of hours from invasion to occupation, and transition toward an economically viable government and ensuring an opportunity for democratization. The Bosnia operations (IFOR) were transformed from a U.N. to a NATO effort and became both peace-enforcement and nation building in a matter of weeks.[4] Kosovo (KFOR) is a mixture of security, humanitarian, and national development that puts military forces into a dynamic and complex role.[5] Afghanistan is following Kosovo in this mission evolution. Efforts by the U.S. Government to support counternarcotics efforts in Colombia and transition countries mix military assets with law enforcement roles and missions. OPERATION IRAQI FREEDOM was simultaneously warfighting, counterinsurgency, and humanitarian operations.

In the 21st century, terrorism has emerged as a major threat to national security, creating a whole new class of military missions accompanied by a new set of capability priorities. Terrorism involves a variety of threats, not just traditional bombs, assassinations, kidnappings, and hostage-taking; it now also includes the threat of weapons of mass destruction. Terrorists or state-sponsored terrorist groups represent chemical, biological, and radiological threats to forces abroad as well as military personnel and facilities within the United States. Military assets may only be capable of countering some types of threats *after* they have been launched, such as the aircraft skyjacked for the September 11, 2001 attacks.[6] Other attacks can be expected to create situations in which the military's superior transportation, communication, and casualty handling capabilities will be needed. In many cases, as in Yemen, Pakistan, and Afghanistan, military capabilities are needed to identify, disrupt, and destroy terrorist organizations and capabilities before they can be employed against U.S. and coalition partner targets. In other cases, such as in the Philippines, training by U.S. military is an important addition to the ability of foreign forces and their law enforcement organizations to locate, disrupt, and destroy terrorist organizations.

Thus, the only way to measure a military's robustness is to examine the effectiveness of C2 systems, operational concepts, and military forces across the full range of operating environments and missions deemed relevant. Figure 18 illustrates one way of organizing this information. The horizontal axis organizes mission types by the roles that the military establishment may play–from combat through monitoring and police activity to support for civilian organizations. The vertical axis describes the nature of the threat entity, from nation-states (Iraq or the Taliban regime in Afghanistan) to subnational actors (Kurds, Palestinians, etc.), to organizations (drug cartels, terrorist organizations without a specific ethnic origin or homeland, rogue arms dealers, and so forth), to individuals (isolated terrorists or individuals organizing attacks), and systemic threats (hurricanes, diseases such as AIDS, or environmental pollution with broad cause and effect).[7]

Two other ways of characterizing threat environments that may also cause them to challenge forces optimized for combat against symmetrical adversaries are (1) the complexity and (2) the duration of the military mission or the conflict. The complexity of military operations needed to deal with a 21st century security environment also challenges traditional military forces. In addition, the response that traditional military forces have optimized for, the threat or application of force in almost any form, will have differential effects, some desirable and others undesirable. Effects-Based Operations[8] are efforts to understand and deal with the complexity of modern missions and their implications for linking military

Mechanism of Engagement

Conflict ← → Cooperation

Traditional Mode of Engagement

	Use of Military Force (Threat or use of US and coalition military force to defend national interests)	Policing / Monitoring (Use of US military to support peacekeeping and complex contingency operations to ensure a secure environment)	Supporting Civilian Missions (Collaboration of US military with civilian entities to further US national interests)
Nation States · Countries · Alliances · Ad hoc coalitions	· Desert Shield/Desert Storm (Iraq) · Uphold Democracy (Haiti)	· UNMIH (Haiti) · Joint Endeavor (Bosnia) · INTERFET (East Timor)	· MIA Recovery Operations
Sub-National Actors · Ethnic groups · Guerrilla groups · Refugees	· Allied Force (Kosovo) · Guardian Retrieval (DRC NEO) · Silver Anvil (Sierra Leone NEO)	· Restore Hope (Somalia) · Joint Guardian (Kosovo) · Essential Harvest (Macedonia)	· Support Hope (Rwanda) · Shining Hope (Kosovo) · Provide Comfort (Kurds)
Organizations · Transnational criminal organizations · Terrorist groups · International business	· Laser Strike (Andean Drug War) · Enduring Freedom (Bin Laden)	· Caribbean Drug Interdiction · Athens Olympic Games security · Internet use to counter terrorist groups	· Noble Eagle (homeland security) · Homeland BW/CW anti-terrorist consequence management
Individuals/Networks · Globalization protestors · Currency speculators · Computer hackers · Migrants	· Maritime interception of new influx of Cuban or Haitian migrants · Special operations to capture terrorist or neutralize a small cell	· Garden Plot (Los Angeles riots) · Capture of CIA Assassin (Kansi) · Globalization protests (WTO, G-8, IMF, etc.)	
Systemic Challenges · Infectious diseases · Natural disasters · Global warming		· Quarantine to control domestic outbreak of Ebola virus	· Fuerte Apoyo (Hurricane Mitch) · Avid Response (Turkey Earthquake) · Forest fire containment (Mexico/Central America)

Emerging Challenges

Figure 18. Future Operational Environment – Security Threat Matrix[9]

actions and operations to diplomatic, information, economic, and social actions.

The duration of the mission also alters the demand for robustness. The operating environment changes over time, which means that the C2 system, operating concepts, and forces will need to prove effective in new and emergent contexts. Even in "pure" military missions, an adversary will learn and adapt over time, representing novel challenges. In other words, the local context for combat will change as new tactics are employed. Robust forces can adjust to these changes. Hence, tactics and techniques that are initially effective will be countered or made less relevant as a campaign proceeds. More commonly, the larger context changes, sometimes creating what is referred to as mission creep, though more realistically these are "mission evolutions." For example, Grenada, Panama, and Haiti began as military missions and then were transformed into security assistance and national development tasks in which the military played a reduced role. Similarly, Bosnia, Kosovo, and Afghanistan have evolved over time. Given that this pattern has repeated itself a number of times, it can now be considered an inherent aspect of a particular class of missions. An agile force is relevant and effective over time despite (1) changes in the way the adversary fights or (2) changes in the fundamental mission.

As indicated before, the proper way to measure the robustness of a force, C2 system, or operating concept is to place them in a variety of contexts. This can be done through a series of historical case studies (not really a useful technique for assessing novel or future capabilities) by creating a set of simulations or artificial environments or through experimentation. *The NATO Code of Best Practice for C2 Assessment*[10] stresses the importance of identifying the range of interesting operating environments or scenarios and selecting particular cases that reflect that range. Then it calls for ensuring that the assessment samples range intelligently. The dimensions that appear most useful for assessing robustness are mission type (nature of objectives, or coalitions), nature of the adversary, complexity, duration, and (to the extent it is not already implied within the other dimensions) size of the operation.

Resilience[11]

Resilience is the ability to recover from or adjust to misfortune, damage, or a destabilizing perturbation in the environment.[12] Military C2 systems and forces are often subjected to attack or asked to perform in challenging environments. Adversaries, particularly asymmetric adversaries, often focus their attacks in ways intended to degrade or make friendly capabilities irrelevant. This includes efforts of adversaries to destroy information through electronic interference, exploit our information by interception, and efforts by adversaries to inflict physical damage on C2 facilities and systems using the means available to them. For example, military organizations will target C2 nodes they perceive to be important while terrorist organizations will attempt to penetrate them with car bombs or other weapons techniques they know how to use; non-national actors can be expected to launch 'denial of service' attacks on rear area nodes that use commercial computers or telecommunications facilities, and so on.

Networks are inherently more resilient than the hierarchical and stovepipe systems that characterized Industrial Age military organizations. Because there are multiple paths available, the loss of a single node or link is absorbed by a robustly networked force. The Internet is a good example of a highly resilient communications system that relies on very simple principles to maintain service even when under considerable stress.[13] The increasing availability of self-healing networks, self-organizing systems, and other technical advances has further enhanced the capacity of networks to function under attack or maintain levels of service despite being comprised of unreliable elements. Military C2 systems cannot achieve the key goal of information assurance[14] unless they are designed for resilience.

Military organizations have always been designed with considerable resilience precisely because they must function in highly lethal environments. The loss of a key node, even a major command center, has traditionally been overcome by having doctrinal solutions, a set of prescribed rules by which command was passed from location to location (for example, from a Division main headquarters to its Tactical headquarters), platform to platform (from a flagship to an alternate vessel), and commander to commander (from the commander to his deputy or most senior subordinate). However, such adjustments have always come at a price, such as time lost while C2 structures are altered and information flows rerouted, a shift of focus as a new commander alters existing plans to reflect his or her individual experience and expertise, and so forth. Fighting forces have relied heavily on redundancy to ensure resilience. When one unit becomes exhausted, it is "rotated" out of line and replaced by another; a platform (tank, aircraft, ship) damaged or destroyed by accident or enemy action is replaced by another. Industrial Age military logistics doctrine was characterized as an "iron mountain," massive quantities of all types of supplies and facilities so that any losses could be replaced or repaired without loss of warfighting momentum.

Information Age approaches to resilience are proving to be much more efficient than those of the last century.[15] First, command centers are at less risk because they are distributed and rely on reachback and reachout to keep many key assets out of harm's way. (Of course, facilities in rear areas must be defended against terrorism, cyber-attacks, and other challenges.) Senior commanders also may well be at less risk because they are more mobile, though many Industrial Age commanders also spent considerable time moving about the battlespace. Second, communications systems are networked, which provides them with greater inherent resilience, and are increasingly characterized by self-organizing and self-healing properties. Third, the use of collaborative decisionmaking not only improves the quality of the decisions expected, but it also ensures a broad and deep understanding of the reasons behind command intent and specific decisions, making it much less likely that the loss of single commander, platform, or unit will disrupt or disorient operations. In addition, by developing richer information and sharing it more broadly, the Information Age force is able to reduce casualties and platform losses, thereby generating greater consistency over time and also enabling the force to learn and retain its learning during engagements, battles, and campaigns. The logistics systems of the Information Age will rely on information, not mass. They will pre-position some assets, distribute others to reduce vulnerability, deliver close to the battlespace, use modular replacement rather than onsite repair, and organize "sense and respond" systems. In this way, they will be following Information Age business practices.

Resilience is also a property of individuals. Research has shown that some individuals "bear up" better under pressure and stress than others. In particular, individuals have been shown to "bounce back" more quickly and more effectively when they can (1) see cause and effect as arising from local conditions rather than global conditions, (2) see themselves as having more control over events than others, and (3) see problems as temporary rather than permanent. This work has proven effective enough that it has been used as a part of personnel selection processes by organizations as diverse as major corporations and professional basketball teams.[16] This research is consistent with military history in which the best commanders refused to give in when events went against them and either found a way to "snatch victory from the jaws of defeat" or extracted their forces from difficult situations so that they were intact to fight again on another day when more favorable initial conditions were possible. Hence, building a resilient force will also involve personnel selection and training issues.

Measuring resilience will require the creation of opportunities to explore the impact of stresses and shocks on the force, the commander, and the systems that support them. As with many important issues, measurement will require establishing some "norm" or baseline condition–the level of performance to be expected under "routine" conditions. This is also a clear case where sampling the interesting and important range of relevant situations or mission capability packages will be essential. No single scenario will be sufficient. Moreover, some scalable way of measuring the strength of the stresses and shocks being administered will also be needed. A more resilient system will be one that can continue to function well under greater stress or stronger shocks. Since stress and shock are inherent in military operations, the "more resilient" commander, force, or systems will be those that (a) can withstand greater pressure and larger shocks and (b) are disrupted for less time. At least one confounding factor must also be considered: the best approaches will be those that avoid stresses and shocks. Hence control needs to be established for this very important factor. Concepts such as stability, convergence, and complexity will provide the basis for measuring resilience.

Finally, resilience is interdependent with other dimensions of agility. In particular, adaptable work processes and organizational structures as well as flexible and innovative decisionmaking will tend to correlate with resilience. The "speed of adjustment" element in resilience will also tend to correlate with responsiveness.

Responsiveness

In some ways, responsiveness is the simplest dimension of agility. It refers to the ability of an operating concept, C2 system, or force to act (or react) effectively in a timely manner. In very high tempo domains, such as air-to-air combat, very brief intervals may be decisive. In more deliberate military domains, such as ground combat, where movement of forces requires more time, responses of minutes (for example, for fires from artillery, rockets, or close air support) or hours (movement, rearming, or preparing defensive positions for ground platforms) may be adequate. For some domains, such as traditional submarine warfare, strategic deployment, or information operations, days or weeks may be the proper tempo. In essence, military actions must be taken within some window of opportunity, which will vary with the situation and the context. Hence, there is no single "optimal" response time.

Speed of response is important, but a rapid incorrect action is not responsive. Both qualities–timeliness and effectiveness–

must be present to conclude that a force, operational concept, or C2 system has been responsive. The defense of Saudi Arabia and the expulsion of Iraqi forces from Kuwait in 1991 make an excellent case in point. When Kuwait fell, the immediate priority for the U.S. and its coalition partners was to ensure the territorial integrity of Saudi Arabia. A combination of rapid deployment (of air power and light forces) and strong diplomatic and information campaigns was instituted very quickly. However, the larger objective of forcing Iraq out of Kuwait was not undertaken immediately because time was needed to create the coalition and force structure required. Had the U.S. and its initial coalition partners launched an early counterattack, they would have done so under less than advantageous circumstances and the risks and costs of the operation (particularly the cost in lives) would very likely have been much higher. By proceeding relatively deliberately, building the coalition, and working through planning alternatives (flexibility: the initial plan was rejected, the forces required were resized, and a new alternative was developed[17]), the U.S.-led coalition was able to select the decisive times, places, and forms of combat. This is the essence of responsiveness: the ability to control tempo, rather than merely the ability to act rapidly.

If Network Centric Warfare was simply an extension of Industrial Age military practices, that would be a sufficient understanding of responsiveness. However, the interrelated ideas of improved shared awareness, increased capacity for sensemaking, faster decisionmaking, more rapid dissemination of command intent and directives (partly due to less use of detailed directives), and more self-synchronized actions mean that responsiveness can be taken to new levels. A true Information Age force is able to create more windows of opportunity (and create them earlier) than its Industrial Age counterpart. Moreover, because its C2 systems and processes allow it to identify more opportunities for synergistic actions (both among elements of the military force and between the elements of that force and civilian organizations), an Information Age force can "hit harder" or generate more momentum toward mission accomplishment than traditional military forces.

Responsiveness of forces is further increased because of their ability to conduct simultaneous and continuous operations— not just hitting harder, but also allowing the adversary less time to build situation awareness and develop countermeasures. In essence, responsiveness means the ability to see more opportunities earlier and to exploit them more quickly, more efficiently, and more effectively. Figure 19 illustrates this principle. Where Industrial Age forces searched for or tried to create an ideal center of gravity in an adversary and developed courses of action and plans that could be exploited (the boxer's targets on left, focused on two vulnerabilities), an Information Age force can see large numbers of vulnerabilities (like the martial artist on right) and take combinations of related actions that both inflict greater damage upon an adversary more rapidly, and also create greater uncertainty for the adversary. If the larger opponent has both flexibility and agility, then he can probably render his greater resources decisive in the field.

Of course, responsiveness is not independent of the other dimensions of agility. For example, both flexibility and innovation in decisionmaking will impact the ability to identify windows of opportunity and ways of exploiting them. Similarly, responsiveness is related to the robustness of a C2 system, operational concept, or force because it is a distribu-

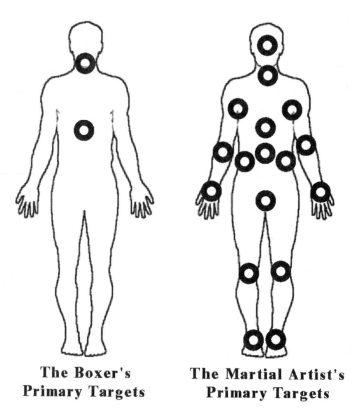

The Boxer's   The Martial Artist's
Primary Targets   Primary Targets

Figure 19. Comparison of Numbers of Targets and Combat Styles: The boxer (left) focuses on the head and torso, while the martial artist (right) finds many more vulnerabilities in the opponent

tion of values across the relevant range of missions and operating environments. Finally, adaptability (changes in organization and work processes) can be expected to increase responsiveness by improving the speed and quality of C2 processes. While we can easily measure one aspect of responsiveness in a particular engagement or campaign by noting (negatively) the frequency with which windows of opportunity are seen but cannot be exploited (one of the classic measures in the HEAT system[18]), and positively in terms of the relative numbers of opportunities identified and exploited by command centers in experiments, a high level of military expertise will be needed to ensure valid and reliable measurement. The overall responsiveness of a C2 system, concept of operations or force will, as with the other dimensions of agility, depend on the distribution of responsiveness across a range of missions and operating contexts.

Flexibility

Flexibility refers to the capability to achieve success in different ways. A flexible C2 system or force is able to generate, consider, and undertake a variety of methods to accomplish its assigned missions. This makes it possible to conduct Effects-Based Operations that employ a variety of synergistic efforts to accomplish a mission efficiently. A flexible force also makes it very difficult for adversaries to find effective courses of action because as they work to foreclose or counter some options, friendly forces are able to shift seamlessly to other alternatives. By doing so, the friendly forces maintain momentum and keep the adversary under pressure, increasing the likelihood of mission accomplishment.

For example, during the early planning for U.S. operations in Afghanistan several different courses of action were identified and teams of analysts and planners were assigned to explore each of them, determine the conditions necessary for their success, and explore how events might unfold over time if they were employed. In the end, the most promising parts of these alternatives were blended into a single, coherent plan. At the same time, the commander and his planning staff retained a rich understanding of the alternative approaches available as the operation unfolded, leaving them with well thought out ideas for alternatives and adjustments as the battlespace changed.

Note that flexibility is primarily an attribute of the cognitive domain. Just as musical geniuses such as Mozart and Beethoven were superior to others in that they had the ability to create more variations on musical themes, so too military genius consists, in part, of the ability to conceptualize more possibilities (tactics or courses of action) than the average commander (Figure 20). This is part of the fundamental difference between ordinary managers in any field and those who are capable of leading major institutions and organizations successfully in times of uncertainty and change.[19] Considerable work has been done that shows that military commanders and other leaders have a strong tendency to exercise "recognition-primed" or "naturalistic" decisionmaking in which they consider only one course of action and rely on their experience

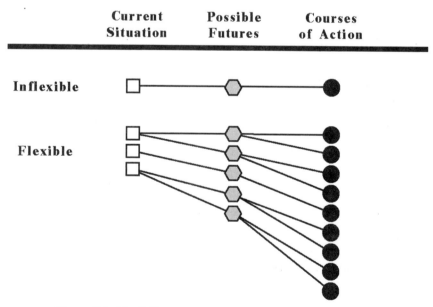

Figure 20. Flexibility creates more options in a given situation

and intuition to guide their decisions.[20] However, this type of decisionmaking is dangerous when (1) the situation is unfamiliar (outside the training and experience of the commander and his key staff), (2) the decision or approach being undertaken is well known to the adversary (predictable and therefore likely to be foreseen and/or countered effectively), or (3) Effects-Based Operations are needed to blend multiple actions (often including nonmilitary actions) into synergistic efforts designed to change the probability of success because the complexity of the situation defies simple linear approaches.

The generation of multiple solutions to a military problem can become an impediment to effective military performance if it becomes an end in itself or causes a military organization to miss important windows of opportunity. However, the agile military command will be characterized by the ability to identify more alternatives in any given situation, and an agile force will be able to implement them efficiently.

Hence, the variety of viable alternative paths to mission accomplishment that can be identified is an indicator of flexibility. The training of commanders and staffs needs to stress mental agility, the ability to see alternatives and the relationships between them. This will be related to their ability to understand the probabilistic nature of complex situations and how to employ Effects-Based Operations to improve the likelihood of success or mission accomplishment.[21]

While the creation of alternatives is a cognitive activity (takes place in an individual's head), that creative process can be stimulated by collaboration among multiple participants, particularly participants who represent genuinely different perspectives. Hence, the social domain is also an important focus for flexibility. Research dating from the 1980s and 1990s on U.S. and NATO commanders indicates a positive correlation between the number of personnel and staff sections participating in course of action and plan development and both the number of alternatives considered and the likelihood of mission success without major revisions to the initial plan.[22] Moreover, the general literature on decisionmaking provides similar findings in domains other than the military. In particular, the tendency for small groups of people to generate narrow views of developing situations and anchor onto a single solution, even in the presence of contrary evidence, has been shown to be a common human failing.[23] Establishing good social networks between commanders and key staff members, both within and across echelons and organizations, is therefore one way to improve flexibility.

Note also that being able to generate more alternatives is not going to be militarily useful unless they can be processed (assessed), perhaps integrated, and certainly put into action by clear and prompt dissemination and implementation. Here again, the social network enabled by a rich set of communications and collaboration tools improves the likelihood of success. Assuming that the process of generating alternatives is a collaborative one (collaboration across echelons, functional areas, interagency partners, and coalition members), the ability to disseminate decisions quickly and the likelihood that they will be understood correctly (for example, that commanders and leaders of all the organizations involved will have congruent intent) can be expected to increase. Similarly, the time available to subordinate organizations is increased because they are aware of the alternatives under analysis and the logic behind them earlier in the process.

Finally, two important capabilities are hiding in the concept of flexibility. The first is the ability for more rapid recognition of changes in the battlespace that may offer new opportunities or threats. What are, in Industrial Age organizations, formal contingency plans and "branches and sequels" that have been neatly articulated and built into formal planning processes and plans need to become, instead, seamless adjustments made by commanders and key staff at all levels as they recognize significant changes in the battlespace. Changes in the situation may involve actions by adversaries or environmental events (for example, bad weather that reduces visibility) that foreclose or marginalize some options or indicate that resources can be freed up or re-employed more effectively. However, the key to flexible implementation is the ability to move seamlessly among options to maintain momentum toward mission accomplishment without having to develop detailed contingency plans. An agile C2 system allows its force to operate a complex, multiple-axis (several synergistic efforts simultaneously and continuously) operation with a coherence that is maintained over time. In other words, it moves the force toward a capability to engage in effective self-synchronization.

The second hidden capability in flexibility is to foresee multiple futures, not just multiple alternative actions. The variety of possible futures is a building block for a rich set of actions. That same variety also serves to reduce the likelihood of surprise. This includes changes in the operating environment, which may be physical (weather), political (coalition issues or changes in the political system of the target), or social (reactions by groups of people in the theater such as refugees or in the international public). In a remarkable number of cases, the adversary has not fully committed to a single course of action. Indeed, the old Soviet doctrine for offensive operations called for a number of probes, followed by commitment of the main effort based on the development of information about weaknesses and opportunities. The adoption of Effects-Based Operations also implies the capability to foresee alternative futures, altering the military and political situations of the adversary in ways that lead to the outcomes we desire.

In terms of measurement, flexibility should be tracked along several dimensions. First, and most simply, the number of genuinely different futures envisioned and alternative courses of action considered by a headquarters or set of headquarters are direct indications of decisionmaking flexibility. There is an upper bound to these values—the seven to nine concepts any one human can retain in conscious memory.[24] However, the tendency of many decisionmakers, including military decisionmakers, to focus in on one understanding of the situation and one course of action means that real command centers are more likely to err on the low side rather than the high side.

The second dimension for measurement and assessment is the number and variety of participants in the development of situation awareness, understandings, and courses of action. While this number and variety are not flexibility in themselves, they are indicators that correlate with flexibility. As discussed earlier, they also increase the likelihood of congruent command intent across echelons, functions, and organizations, which implies not only more rigorous thinking but also more rapid and more effective dissemination and implementation.

A third related dimension is the use of collaborative processes for the elements of sensemaking (situation awareness and understandings) as well as decisionmaking with respect to courses of action and planning. Here again, flexibility is not guaranteed by the use of collaborative work processes, but its likelihood increases when the key participants have the opportunity to interact.

Flexibility is also measurable in terms of the structure of the actions undertaken by the force. Flexible sets of actions include more than one path to success. Moreover, those sets of actions tend to be synergistic, combing to form effects greater than those they would achieve if they were undertaken individually. In other words, there is a natural correlation between flexibility and Effects-Based Operations.

Innovation

Innovation is the ability to do things in new ways or to undertake new things to do, particularly new ways to achieve desired ends. This involves the ability to learn over time (across missions or engagements during a campaign) about missions and operational environments and to take advantage of the lessons learned to create and maintain competitive advantages. No matter how many times a task or mission has successfully been accomplished, nor how flexible the C2 systems and processes are, creative changes will be needed in any sustained operation in order to exploit opportunities, avoid predictability, avoid emerging threats, and keep the adversary off balance and highly uncertain. Similarly, operational experiences should be mined for lessons learned and patterns that might be exploited by the next adversary. Adversaries learn over time and across operations. It cannot be assumed that they will act/react in the same way the next time. Innovation denies them advantage from their learning and confounds their efforts to take advantage of their knowledge of our doctrine, tactics, techniques, and procedures.

The following two examples of U.S. failures illustrate the importance of being innovative in today's threat environment. The destruction of the U.S. Marine Corps barracks in Beirut in 1983 was accomplished by a suicide bomber (Figure 21). Although the barracks were defended extensively with barriers and armed guards, the defenses were static. They were not changed for weeks preceding the attack. That fact, and the fact that the defenses were in the open and could be seen, allowed the group planning the attack to construct a replica of those defenses. This was used for practice, so the driver of the truck carrying the explosives had considerable experience in driving the precise route needed to reach the barracks. Had there been some randomness in the defenses (changing the pattern of barriers, changing the location of the guards, etc.), the probability that the truck bomb would have been successful would have been reduced.[25] This terrorist attack had a significant impact on U.S. policy in the Middle East. Its success remains an important lesson in the continuing need for innovation.

The other example is the "Ranger Raid" in Mogadishu in 1993. In this case, the same tactics and techniques were employed in several consecutive raids by the U.S. Rangers.[26] As a consequence, the Somali forces were able to identify and prepare a response that focused their advantages (rocket propelled grenades against helicopters and massed forces willing to accept massive casualties) to offset the superior firepower and maneuver advantages of the U.S. and its U.N. coalition partners.

U.S. forces have certainly employed innovation effectively. This has been one of their hallmarks over time, and has frustrated enemy commanders who sought to understand American tactics.[27] The use of an aircraft carrier as a platform

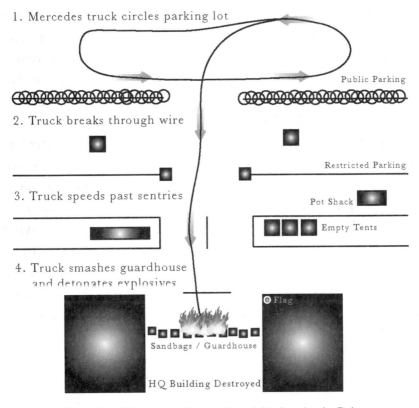

1. Mercedes truck circles parking lot

Public Parking

2. Truck breaks through wire

Restricted Parking

3. Truck speeds past sentries

Pot Shack

Empty Tents

4. Truck smashes guardhouse and detonates explosives

Flag

Sandbags / Guardhouse

HQ Building Destroyed

Figure 21. The route taken by the suicide bomber in Beirut

for Army assets during the operation in Haiti in October of 1983 is an excellent example. Similarly, the "Hail Mary" around the Iraqi left flank during the Gulf War I ground war caught the enemy by surprise, as did the U.S. decision not to launch an amphibious assault. Deception and concentrated efforts to disrupt Iraqi intelligence proved highly effective. While the full story is not well documented at this writing, U.S. forces were also highly innovative during the invasion of Afghanistan, bringing precision weapons to bear on an adversary unprepared for their employment. The tactics, techniques, and procedures employed were, in large measure, developed in the field and employed novel linkages between sensors, forces in the field, and shooters.

Measuring Innovation

Recognizing and measuring innovation reliably and validly will be a challenge. The measurement of creativity, which is what is needed here, is difficult under the best of circumstances. No automatic system is likely to be developed except in heavily structured parts of military operations (routine logistics, ISR planning, etc.). The only general solution will probably involve using experts (which can be tricky since their expertise usually focuses on orthodoxy and established norms) with structured instruments of observation and questionnaires. The experts in such a system essentially represent knowledge of the routine and doctrinal approaches to military problems. In naturally conservative institutions such as DoD and the Services, novel approaches are seldom readily appreciated, precisely because the established way of doing business has been designed for "optimal" performance in the anticipated combat environment. The establishment recognizes and rewards those who follow such doctrine. This, of course, is precisely why military genius succeeds–the actions taken are unexpected by the adversary's commanders.

Research into existing approaches and instruments for assessing creativity is an important priority. Relatively little work has been done on recognizing and grading innovation (what is "a little bit" creative? "more" creative? etc.) in the military context. The creative component of work in the creative arts is often judged by experts, who often disagree about the value of new approaches. The use of simulation may help here because innovations can be tried and some indications of their potential can be ascertained.

While difficult to recognize and measure, innovation is crucial in C2, forces, and concepts of operation. Avoiding predictability is clearly an essential element of agility. It can provide an important competitive edge in a wide range of missions, from peacekeeping to major combat. We need a better understanding of what innovation is in a military campaign, how to measure it, and how to teach and encourage it.

Adaptation

Adaptation is the ability to alter force organization and work processes when necessary as the situation and/or environment changes.[28] Where the other elements of agility are focused outward, adaptation is focused inward. However, it is not unrelated to those other elements. The capacity to change the organization and business rules by which we operate can make us more effective and efficient when dealing with different types of missions. This capacity also makes it more likely that we can be responsive, flexible, and innovative across new and emerging 21st century situations because it frees us from roles, doctrines, and practices that were designed and developed to work against the threats of the 20th (and even 19th) century.

Adaptive organizations (1) alter the way information is distributed and involve different participants in collaboration or planning sessions based on changes in the operating environment, (2) create new ways of dealing with coalition, interagency, and nongovernmental partners, (3) flatten organizational structures, and (4) develop and adapt more efficient work processes based on experience over time. Indeed, we cannot (and should not presume to) identify all the changes to the way we approach and accomplish missions that will be needed for future situations. Rather, we need to enable those who will organize and command future forces to reorganize and reallocate functions as they see fit. We also need to seek ways to achieve a degree of self-organization.

The new networks (relationships) of sensors, ground forces, and shooters that arose during U.S. operations in Afghanistan are examples of the types of adaptation that produce agility. The evolution of command arrangements in peace operations, including the development of civil-military operations centers, is a similar development.[29] The concept of integration across function, echelon, and organization, which is crucial to Network Centric Warfare, involves major changes in organization and work processes. Moreover, the concept of tailored task forces, which has proven very effective over time, is an excellent example of force adaptation based on missions.

In excellent but often overlooked research on U.S. Army Brigade command centers, Olmstead[30] demonstrated that the best of those commands actually changed their internal work processes during exercises. They recognized the difference between planning-intensive phases, when they had the luxury of time and could work a formal staff process, and those times when the unit was heavily engaged and needed to work more quickly and efficiently. Hayes[31] found that theater level command centers during World War II altered their internal structure (increasing the proportion of personnel in intelligence, while reducing the number in operations) as they gained combat experience.[32] Moreover, many of those headquarters made these changes informally long before they altered their organization charts. The argument also emerged in that research that a failure of the German Army to make a similar change was one of the factors contributing to their declining performance over time during World War II. Finally, research on post-Cold War U.S. Army command centers showed shifting attention (from heavier on Red to heavier on Blue) and time horizons for situation assessment (shortening) during periods of heavy engagement. These patterns are consistent with research on the psychology of decisionmaking, which predicts that people will alter their attention to focus on the familiar when they are under stress.

Perhaps the most explicit example of organizational adaptation is the concept of a modular command center put forward by Marine General Anthony Charles Zinni, former CENT-COM commander and one of the most experienced U.S. leaders in a variety of military contexts. His concept involved *layers* of staff members (a few key people in the inner circle, several leaders of staff sections in a second layer, and staff sections in the outer layer) and selected staff functions chosen because of the nature of the military mission and the role of the military in a larger (international) context.[33] Zinni recognized that the commander needs only a few staff sections in order to command and control low threat, humanitarian missions, more to handle peace operations (which vary according to the likelihood that the parties will threaten or attack one another or the peacekeepers), and still more in major combat. Moreover, the importance of various functions will vary–lawyers, doctors, logisticians, civil-military specialists, military police, the political advisor function, and information (media) specialists may form the major sections in a humanitarian operation. Hence, the classic Napoleonic staff codes are of limited utility and suggest a very different profile from the one the command requires for success in these particular missions. Zinni's reliance on a few key staff members and a few sections, both selected to deal with the particular problems at hand, implies considerable effectiveness as well as adaptation when compared with Industrial Age militaries.

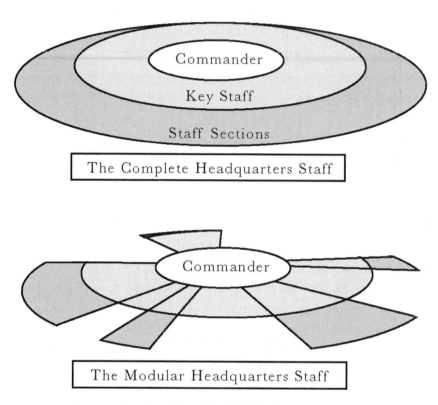

Figure 22. General Zinni's Modular Commander Center

This type of modular approach has also been raised in the discussions about how to create and use Standing Joint Force Headquarters. The Chairman of the Joint Chiefs of Staff has mandated that these be created within every Regional Combat Command (RCC) in the year 2005.[34] However, how these entities are organized, staffed, and used is an open question, with various employment models offered, including:

- Using the SJFHQ as the core of a larger headquarters;

- Splitting the SJFHQ so that some of it remains at the RCC and some of it goes forward with the larger headquarters;

- Spreading the SJFHQ out across the elements of the larger headquarters; or

- Keeping the SJFHQ at the RCC while a larger head-quarters goes forward.

Similarly, the concepts of reachback and reachout imply that smaller forward headquarters will rely on staff elements not in the operational theater to perform many functions, which reduces footprint and vulnerability. The decision of the CEN-TCOM commander to keep his major headquarters in Florida and create a "coalition village" there during OPERATION ENDURING FREEDOM in Afghanistan represents a major departure from past practice, creating a new organization and work process adapted to the demands of that conflict.

At the level of adaptable forces, the concept of tailored task forces has been around for a very long time. U.S. doctrine recognizes that different combat missions require different force mixes. Hence, it is quite normal to see combat organizations augmented with key elements intended to increase their relevant capabilities. For example, organizations that are tasked to build or breach fortifications are typically augmented with engineering units. During the planning for Gulf War I, the need to increase the heavy armor capacity of the USMC Division attacking directly into Kuwait was handled by assigning a U.S. Army Brigade made up of M1A1 Tanks.[35] U.S. Navy forces typically design specific task forces for each mission, deleting assets that are seen as unnecessary and adding assets (such as air defense, countermine capabilities, or attack submarines) likely to increase the probability of mission success. Future agile forces are likely to be composed of units that can be rapidly brought together to accomplish specific missions or achieve specific objectives, then reorganized or reconfigured to take on new responsibilities. This implies a high degree of interoperability across force elements and units.

The Network Centric Warfare concept of self-synchronizing forces is a statement of the requirement for massive improvements not only in flexibility but also in adaptability. The elements of such forces will need to be extremely competent and inspire confidence in the other force elements about that competence. They will also have to trust one another, recognizing the value of synergistic efforts and their ability to rely on one another to achieve them. They will need to be supported by networks that allow them not only to share information but also the tools that they need to develop situation awareness and situation understanding. They will also need to task reorganize on the fly.

NCW implies command and control structures and processes that are highly adaptable. This means that they will need to be modular, be able to incorporate new actors rapidly and efficiently, employ reachback and reachout as part of their natural C2 functions, be able to make decisions very rapidly when decisively engaged, but retain control of the pace of battle when the time is available to develop richer understandings and approaches to success, and also be able to forecast and recognize changes in the battlespace quickly.

Measurement of adaptation will not be easy. However, some indicators will be easy to recognize such as formal shifts in

organizational structures, explicit alterations in work processes, and changes in communications patterns. However,
most of these changes will be difficult to measure beyond an
ordinal level. Informal changes in work processes will be more
difficult to recognize without expert observation or participant
reporting. However, sociologists and other social scientists
have developed observation and scaling techniques in the
world of business and decisionmaking under stress that can be
adapted to those purposes.[36]

NOTES

1   Sun Tzu. Thomas Cleary trans. *The Art of War*. Boston: Shambhala
    Publications, Inc. 1991.

2   Attrition-based, rather than effects-based.

3   Alberts, *Command Arrangements*.
    Davidson, Lisa Witzig, Margaret Daly Hayes, and James J. Landon.
    Humanitarian and Peace Operations: NGOs and the Military in the Interagency Process.
    Washington, DC: CCRP Publication Series. December 1996.

4   "The Bosnia-Herzegovina After Action Review I (BHAAR I) Conference
    Report." Carlisle Barracks, PA: United States Army Peacekeeping Institute
    (PKI). May 20-23, 1996.
    http://www.au.af.mil/au/awc/awcgate/lessons/bhaar1.htm. (May 1,
    2003)

5   Ministry of Defence. "Kosovo: Lessons from the Crisis." Presented to
    Parliament by the Secretary of State for Defence by Command of Her
    Majesty. June 2000.
    http://www.mod.uk/publications/kosovo_lessons/contents.htm. (May 1,
    2003)
    Gallis, Paul E. "Kosovo: Lessons Learned from Operation *Allied Force*."
    Congressional Research Service Report to Congress, The Library of
    Congress. November 19, 1999.
    http://www.au.af.mil/au/awc/awcgate/crs/rl30374.pdf. (May 1, 2003)

6   Bush, President George W. "Statement by the President in his Address to the
    Nation." Office of the Press Secretary. September 11, 2001.
    http://www.whitehouse.gov/news/releases/2001/09/20010911-16.html.
    (May 1, 2003)

7   Bush, President George W. "The National Security Strategy of the United States of America." White House. September 2002. http://www.whitehouse.gov/nsc/nss.pdf. (May 1, 2003)

8   Smith, *Effects*.

9   Adapted from original work by Randolph Pherson.

10 NATO SAS026. *NATO Code of Best Practice for C2 Assessment*. Washington, DC: CCRP Publication Series. 2003.

11 *Bell, Chip R.* "Picking Super Service Personnel." *Supervisory Management.* Vol 35, Iss 6. Saranac Lake. Jun 1990. p. 6.
    Coutu, Diane L. "How Resilience Works." *Harvard Business Review.* Boston, MA: Harvard Business School Press. May 2002.
    Weick, Karl E. "The Collapse of Sensemaking in Organizations: The Mann Gulch Disaster." *Administrative Science Quarterly.* Ithaca. Dec 1993.

12 Adapted from: *Merriam Webster's Collegiate® Dictionary, 10th Edition.* Springfield, MA: Merriam-Webster, Inc. 1998.

13 Even Internet-giant Microsoft has fallen prey to such stress in the form of "denial of service" attacks.
    Fontana, John. "Denial-of-service attacks cripple Microsoft for second day." *NetworkWorldFusion.* January 25, 2001.

14 Carley, Kathleen M., Ju-Sung Lee, and David Krackhardt. "Destabilizing Networks." *Connections.* No 24(3): 79-92. British Colombia, CAN: INSNA. 2002.

15 Lewandowski, CAPT Linda. *Sense and Respond Logistics: The Fundamentals of Demand Networks.* U.S. Navy Office of the Secretary of Defense, Office of Force Transformation. Jeffrey R. Cares Alidade Incorporated. 2002.

16 Greenberg, Jeanne and Herbert M., Ph.D. "The Personality Of A Top Salesperson." *Nation's Business.* December, 1983.

17 Petre, Peter. *General Norman Schwarzkopf: It Doesn't Take a Hero.* New York, NY: Banton Books. 1992. p. 451.

18 Hayes, Richard E., Mark Hainline, Conrad Strack, and Daniel Bucioni. "HEAT measures for Decision Cycle Time, Lead Time to Subordinates and Plan Quality, from Defense Systems, Inc." *Theater Headquarters Effectiveness: It's Measurement and Relationship to Size Structure, Functions, and Linkage.* McLean, VA: Defense Systems, Inc. 1983.

19 Jaques, Elliot. *Social Power and the CEO: Leadership and Trust in a Sustainable Free Enterprise System.* Westport, CT: Greenwood Publishing Group. 2002.
    Jaques, Elliot. *A General Theory of Bureaucracy.* Hoboken, NJ: John Wiley &

Sons. 1976. Bohnenberger, Thorsten. "Recommendation Planning under Uncertainty: Consequences of Inaccurate Probabilities." Department of Computer Science, Saarland University. 2001. http://orgwis.gmd.de/~gross/um2001ws/papers/position_papers/ bohnenberger.pdf. (Apr 1, 2003)

James, John, Brian Sayrs, V. S. Subrahmanian, and John Benton "Uncertainty Management: Keeping Battlespace Visualization Honest." http://www.atl.external.lmco.com/overview/papers/951-9864a.pdf. (Apr 1, 2003)

Smith, Preston G. *Managing Risk Proactively in Product Development Projects.* Portland, OR: New Product Dynamics. 2002. http://www.newproductdynamics.com/Risk/IPL921.pdf. (Apr 1, 2003)

20 Klein, Gary. *Why Developing Your Gut Instincts Will Make You Better at What You Do.* New York, NY: Doubleday and Company, INC. 2002.
Klein, Gary and Eduardo Salas. *Linking Expertise and Naturalistic Decision Making.* Mahwah, NJ: Lawrence Erlbaum Assoc. 2001.

21 Hayes, Richard, and Sue Iwanski. "Analyzing Effects Based Operations (EBO) Workshop Summary." *Phalanx.* Alexandria, VA: MORS. March 2002. Vol 35, No 1. p. 1.

22 U.S. Army Research Institute for the Behavioral and Social Sciences. *The Army Command and Control Evaluation System Documentation.* Fort Leavenworth Research Unit. 1995.

23 Dixon, Norman F. *On the Psychology of Military Incompetence.* New York: Basic Books. 1976.
As defined by Allyn & Bacon / Longman: Groupthink is a concept that refers to faulty decisionmaking in a group. Groups experiencing groupthink do not consider all alternatives and they desire unanimity at the expense of quality decisions.
Janis, Irving. *Groupthink: Psychological Studies of Policy Decisions and Fiascoes.* Boston, MA: Houghton Mifflin College. 1982.

24 Kalat, J. W. *Biological Psychology* (6th ed.). Pacific Grove, CA: Brooks/Cole. 1998.
Miller, G.A. "The magical number seven, plus or minus two: Some limits on our capacity for processing information." *The Psychological Review.* Vol. 63. 1956. pp. 81-97.

25 *Report of the DoD Commission on Beirut International Airport Terrorist Act, October 23, 1983.* The Long Commission Report. 1983.
"Who is to Blame for the Bombing?" *New York Times.* Aug. 11, 1985.

http://www.ibiblio.org/hyperwar/AMH/XX/MidEast/Lebanon-1982-1984/DOD-Report/index.html (Feb 1, 2003)

26 Bowden, Mark. *Black Hawk Down: A Story of Modern War*. New York, NY: Penguin. 2000.
Somalia Inquiry Report. Department of National Defence, CA. 1997.
http://www.dnd.ca/somalia/somaliae.htm (Feb 1, 2003)

27 "The most difficult thing about planning against the Americans is that they do not read their own doctrine, and they would feel no particular obligation to follow it if they did." -Admiral Sergei I. Gorshkov, father of the Russian blue water navy.

28 We are using adaptation in a different sense than it is used in biological evolution. Darwinian evolution is about the fitness of the individual members of a species for the environment. Those best fit to survive with superior adaptive abilities dominate the environment over time. Our use involves conscious change.

29 Alberts, *Command Arrangements*.

30 Olmstead, J.A., M.J. Baranick and B.L. Elder. *Research on Training for Brigade Command Groups: Factors Contributing to Unit Combat Readiness (Technical Report TR-78-A18)*. Alexandria, VA: U.S. Army Research Institute. 1978.

31 Hayes, Richard E., Mark Hainline, Conrad Strack, and Daniel Bucioni. *Theater Headquarters Effectiveness: It's Measurement and Relationship to Size Structure, Functions, and Linkage*. McLean, VA: Defense Systems, Inc. 1983.
Defense Systems, Inc. *Headquarters Effectiveness Program Summary Task 002*. Arlington, VA: C3 Architecture and Mission Analysis, Planning and Systems Integration Directorate, Defense Communications Agency. 1983.

32 JO99 and the changes in organization that allowed the team to be successful in hunting SCUDs also mention that 2 groups found different ways to organize that were effective. Hence there is no right answer.

33 Wykoff, Maj Michael D. "Shrinking the JTF Staff: Can We Reduce the Footprint Ashore?" Fort Leavenworth, KS.: School of Advanced Military Studies, Command and General Staff College. 1996.
Rinaldo, Richard. "Peace Operations: Perceptions." *A Common Perspective*. Joint Warfighting Center. Vol 7, No 2. 1999.

34 Statement Of Admiral Edmund P. Giambastiani, Jr. Commander United States Joint Forces Command Before The House Armed Services Committee United States House Of Representatives. March 12, 2003.
http://www.jfcom.mil/newslink/storyarchive/2003/pa031203.htm. (Apr 1, 2003)

35 A total of 76 U.S. Army M1A1 tanks were employed by the Marine Corps
    2nd Tank Battalion and elements of the 4th Tank Battalion during
    Operation Desert Storm.
    http://www.hqmc.usmc.mil/factfile.nsf/
    7e931335d515626a8525628100676e0c/
    9e6cdb7ba648f1388525627b0065de66?OpenDocument (Feb 1, 2003)

36 Wall, Toby D., Paul R. Jackson, Sean Mullarkey, and Sharon K Parker.
    "The demands-control model of job strain: A more specific test." Leicester,
    UK: Journal of Occupational and Organizational Psychology. June 1996.
    Rettinger, David A., and Reid Hastie. "Content effects on decision making."
    Organizational Behavior and Human Decision Processes. New York. Jul 2001.

Chapter 9

Power and the Edge

This chapter introduces the basic concepts associated with *power to the edge,* an inherently Information Age approach to organization. When *power to the edge* concepts are applied to command and control and its supporting infostructure,[1] military organizations will be able to overcome the shortcomings of their Industrial Age predecessors and develop the interoperability and agility necessary for success. We begin by looking at what constitutes *power* in an organization and how power is distributed in traditional hierarchies. The concept of the *edge* of an organization is introduced and related to an organization's topology of power. With both *power* and the *edge* defined in the context of military organizations, the basic building blocks for a new approach to military command and control, suitable for the challenges of the 21st century, will have been introduced.

POWER

The word *power* has one of the longest definitions in the dictionary.[2] This is because power has an instantiation in many domains. Power has meaning in the physical, information, social, political, economic, and, of course, the military domains. Power is a concept that applies to people, teams, organizations, coalitions, countries, machines, and objects of wealth such as fuels and information.

In physics, power is about moving objects. In electricity, power is about moving current. In the social and political domains, power is about influence. Power in economics involves wealth creation, while in the military domain it often involves selective destruction. All concepts of power involve the extent of an accomplishment in the face of some measure of resistance.

Power has also been defined as "the ability to influence others to believe, behave, or to value as those in power desire."[3] Power, in the social domain, is a force that allows those "in power" to organize and motivate others to accomplish desired tasks. In organizations, individuals or groups of individuals manifest many different aspects of power, including the power to influence, to organize, to reward, and to accomplish a task.

To first order, power is the ability to make something happen. The amount of power is expressed as a vector. Its components include (1) the magnitude of the accomplishment, (2) the amount of opposition, and (3) the time required.

Power derives from a number of different sources. These include wealth, expertise, delegation (e.g., the power of elected representatives) and, of course, information.

Exercising power requires two fundamental prerequisites: means and opportunity. Available means are not necessarily available for everyone in an organization. In fact, functional specialization is the distribution of means. Access to means is usually the result of an allocation of resources. Often the means required involve an orchestration of multiple individuals and/or organizations. In the case of information, it is access that needs to be provided. Information from multiple sources and/or analyses involving multiple perspectives and/or expertise is often required. Opportunity is a function of (1) the authority to act and (2) circumstances. Circumstances often involve opportunities that are fleeting and one must be able to act individually or in concert with others by a given point in time. Power is therefore something that can, in part, be delegated.

The way that an organization exercises power, indeed the power of an organization, depends as much upon the way it is organized as the totality of its means and the information that is available.

Military Power in the Industrial Age

Military platforms have come to symbolize military power. This Industrial Age association persists despite the fact that the relative value of platforms is rapidly diminishing. The NCW Report to Congress concluded that, "in the future, the network will be the single most important contributor to combat power."[4] This conclusion follows from both the fundamental changes that are associated with the ongoing Revolutions in Security Affairs (RSA) and Military Affairs (RMA).[5]

The RSA means that there will be fewer occasions when the ability to kill large numbers of people or cause massive destruction will be useful, particularly when there is significant collateral damage. However, it will always be important to be able to apply force with precision to destroy or disable an adversary capability and disrupt that adversary's plans. In addition, there will be a host of capabilities that have nothing to do with kinetic force that will be needed to conduct military operations. Our current symbols of power are platforms, which are large, costly affairs, optimized for firepower, survivability, and maneuverability and designed to attrit the capabilities of a symmetric adversary. They are also very blunt instruments. Their effects can be quite indiscriminate, making them politically unusable in many situations. Being large and being manned also makes it important that they there are well protected. This creates a large footprint and increases the risks involved. This also sometimes makes us reluctant to employ them in situations where (a) they are at risk or (b) collateral damage is expected to undermine our efforts. In other situations, it dictates that we must first act to significantly reduce the risks by "preparing the battlefield." For example, in order to reduce the risk associated with using certain air assets, we conduct SEAD[6] missions. This takes time and involves some expenditure, and also results in some lost opportunities. These facts have not escaped the attention of our adversaries. The net result is that over time we can expect that the value of these Industrial Age artifacts will continue to diminish.

Platforms in the Information Age

Fortunately, both the purpose and the physical attributes of platforms are already in the early stages of a profound transformation. These platforms once relied solely upon their organic information assets. Today, they increasingly rely heavily on the network for targeting priorities and information. In Gulf War I (1991), target assignments for planes were made in advance of takeoff. In Gulf War II (2003), many planes received their target information "just in time." This increases agility.

In the future, platforms will evolve from being networked entities to being nodes in the network, to organizing efforts resembling "packs"[7] and "swarms." This transformation will be so complete that the packs and swarms that evolve from existing platforms will bear no resemblance to their distant (in generations, not time) predecessors. Hence, in the process, the very notion of a platform will evaporate; their raison d'etre will be satisfied by a new approach as a result of a series of transformations consisting of ever-larger numbers of smaller, dumber, and cheaper components. These collections of entities will ultimately become dynamically reconfigurable packs, swarms, or other organizations of highly specialized components that work together like the cells of our bodies. As such, they will be able to be far more discriminating and precise in the effects they cause. They will become less mechanical and more organic, less engineered and more "grown."

For years now, the symbolic value of platforms has served to divert our attention from a much-needed fundamental re-examination of power in military organizations. NCW is a break with this Industrial Age past. In asserting the fundamental power of the network rather than its constituent nodes, NCW began a re-examination of the concept of power in military organizations. Early manifestations of NCW capabilities have marked the beginning of power moving to the edge, which is necessary for NCW to become fully mature. Thus, *power to the edge* is the principle that needs to be applied to enable NCW to reach its full potential.

New Means and New Opportunities

The power (firepower) that has been associated with platforms is an expression of means, while its maneuverability has been an expression of opportunity. Until very recently, consideration of both was limited mainly to the physical domain. However, power has meaning in each of the other three domains (information, cognitive, and social) of the NCW Conceptual Framework. Figure 23 identifies the sources of power and maps them to the four domains.

	Means	Opportunity
Physical	Organic Resources	The right actions The right places at the right times
Information	Organic Information	The right information at the right time
Cognitive	Knowledge and ability	The right understandings at the right time
Social	Access to information	The right rules of engagement and partners at the right time
	Command Authority	The right distribution of command intent at the right time

Figure 23. The Sources of Power as a Function of Domain

The extent to which these sources of power exist for force entities varies as a function of the characteristics of the mission capability packages.[8] For example, the material part of the MCP determines the nature of the resources available while organization determines how these resources are allocated. System characteristics determine what information processing and exchanges are possible while doctrine determines access, the actual flows, and the nature of the interactions among entities. Education and training determine what knowledge and abilities the people in the entities have. The command and control approach determines entities' command authority and the approach that is taken to control.

Being at the right place at the right time is a function of more than equipment capabilities that enable one to get to the right place in time. It is also a function of knowing where the right place is, what the right time is, and having the authority to be able to position oneself. Most of all, it is a function of being able to create opportunities, to shape the battle. Being able to get the right information in a timely manner is a function of information availability, network topology and performance, information management capabilities, and information dissemination policy.

Drawing the correct inferences from available information is a function of the a priori knowledge and expertise that can be brought to bear. These in turn are a function of who participates in the organizational processes that develop situation awareness. Entities that have the means to act and find themselves in a position to act still need the authority to act. Hence, rules of engagement also need to be appropriately permissive and appropriate partners are needed.

Power, the potential to make something happen, requires the confluence of many factors across the domains. Many of these factors are intangible (e.g., how well an individual, group, organization, enterprise, or coalition utilizes available information; how command is provided; and how control is exercised). Thus, given a set of material capabilities (tangible sources of power), the power that can be generated by an organization can vary widely as a function of the intangibles (e.g., principles of organization and work process adaptation).

Nature of Power in the Information Age

In the Information Age, power as it is defined here is in part a normal commodity that has a significant marginal cost associated with extra units, and in part a commodity like information that can be "replicated" at an insignificant marginal cost. In some instances, the replication of information actually has a negative cost. When power is related to tangible resources (e.g., people, machines, consumables), it behaves like any commodity. But when the intangible sources of power are factored in, it behaves more like information (which is one of the intangible contributors to power). Hence, the changes in the economics of information that spawned the Information Age lead us to the principle of *power to the edge* as well.

This means that an organization's power can be increased without significant resource expenditures. It can be increased by changing the way we command, control, organize, train, equip, and fight. *Power to the edge* can increase the power of an organization or a system by (1) increasing the power of edge entities and (2) increasing the percentage of entities that are empowered. This is accomplished by increasing an entity's means and/or its opportunities.

An organization's power is also a function of the power of its members[9] and the nature of the interactions among those members.[10] Organizations realize their potential power by instantiating mission capability packages. The ability of an organization to assemble, field, and adapt MCPs determines its power. Hence, the power of the organization is greater than the sum of the power of the organization's individual members. That is only one of the independent variables in the equation. The key to an organization's power rests in how the capabilities of its constituent parts are leveraged, that is, the synergies that are developed. This is the logic behind the emphasis that NCW places on the ability to self-synchronize.

THE EDGE

In common usage, the word *edge* refers to the cutting part of a blade, a sharpness of voice, an extreme position, the brink of something, an advantage, or a boundary. Boundaries are meaningful only in the context of a topology. A topology is defined by those factors that determine the distribution or location of entities within the space of the topology. Thus, the meaning of *the edge* depends upon the organizing principle of the topology in question. In an Industrial Age organization, being at the edge can mean being (1) far from the center, at the "pointy end of the spear" (2) lowest in rank, or (3) in contact with the customer. Paradoxically, the first two are associated with a lack of power while the third is focused on the ability to make things happen. Often, the phrase "pointy end of the spear" is used to distinguish a critical mission (line function) from a supporting (or overhead) activity. This distinction is no longer useful because all of these functions are now integral to operations. For example, information/analytic functions were not considered to be at the pointy end of the spear. Now they provide, sometimes in real time, crucial information such as coordinates that are needed to guide ordinance to their targets (information is now literally at the pointy end of the spear).

In a hierarchical organization, one with a topology organized by status and power, those at the top are at the center and those at the bottom are at the edge. In addition, there is a significant portion of the organization in the middle. Those at the top have the power to command, to set the direction for the organization, allocate its resources, and control the reward structure. Information flows along the axes of power, hence these flows are vertical. Information collected at the bottom flows vertically to the top, and directives flow vertically from the top to the bottom. The middle is needed to deal with the practical limits on span of control. The middle serves to mediate and interpret information flows in both directions, allocate resources, and delegate authority. Some think of the top as exercising command and the middle as exercising control.

But hierarchies are seldom monolithic. Hierarchies are commonly composed of specialized stovepipes that balkanize the organization, creating fiefdoms that are difficult to meld into a coherent whole. Organizational stovepipes are created, differentiated, and sustained as a result of (1) the channeling of communications up and down the chain of command, (2) the tendency for loyalty to be localized, and (3) the lack of systems that support widespread information sharing and peer-to-peer interactions. The result is not a single center but a loose confederation of centers, not one edge but many. Stovepipes greatly inhibit information flows, constrain command approaches, and restrict asset utilization. Stovepipes suboptimize. Worst of all, stovepipes result in cultural differences and tensions between and among different parts of the organization.

Senior managers interested in improving organizational performance have explored ways to increase cross-talk, interoperability, and collaboration among the organization's constituent parts. This effort has proven to be difficult because organizational structure and culture are often working against them. The improvements that they have achieved have often been at great personal expense, only to be short-lived.

In the Industrial Age, stovepipes were necessary because the economics of information made it prohibitively costly to support widespread information sharing and peer-to-peer interactions. With the advent of networking, the economics of information have changed. Senior managers now have an opportunity to remove a major impediment to information sharing and collaboration. Investment in a robust ubiquitous network can eliminate a major source of friction and a lack of system connectivity and interoperability. This makes stovepipes unnecessary.

This is fortunate because with the changing nature of the security environment, particularly the increased importance on noncombat and coalition missions, the problems military organizations face and the nature of the tasks undertaken have grown in complexity and require ever more rapid responses. Constraints on information flows prevent the timely development of situation awareness while constraints on command approach and asset utilization make it more difficult to respond appropriately and/or rapidly.

The adverse affects of stovepipes often come to light as a result of a catastrophic failure. In hindsight, the failure to predict and prevent the tragedy of September 11, 2001, has been attributed to the failure of law enforcement and intelligence community stovepipes to share information and collaborate effectively.[11] Some have proposed centralized solutions to this problem. They will not work. The only way to ensure that information will be shared and that individuals and organizations will work together appropriately is to move power to the edge.

However, stovepipes continue to persist despite the fact that they are no longer technically necessary. This is largely the result of residual organizational and cultural issues. But proofs of concept for a different approach abound.

Information Age technologies have enabled the flattening of organizations and the creation of virtual organizations that redefine the relationships within an organization, and the development of new business models that redefine the relationships among organizations and/or individuals and organizations in a competitive space.[12] The hierarchical organization is a centralized status-power topology with its small but powerful center, a significant middle that serves to operationalize command and exercise control, and an edge that has very limited means and opportunity (power).

The traditional hierarchy is no longer the only game in town for militaries. A new kind of organization, an *edge organization*, has been enabled by a change in the power proposition for information. Edge organizations are characterized by the widespread sharing of information and the predominance of peer-to-peer relationships. Edge organizations have a fundamentally different power topology from traditional organizations. In an edge organization, virtually everyone is at the edge because they are empowered. The distinctions between line and support organizations disappear. The resulting stovepipes, associated with separating line from support organizations, are eliminated as well. The need for the communications and translation functions performed by the middle is greatly diminished and as that need diminishes so will the size of the middle. With the disappearance of stovepipes and the demise of the middle, barriers to information sharing and collaboration disappear as well. Edge organizations are, in fact, collaborative organizations that are inclusive, as opposed to hierarchies that are authoritarian and exclusive. In socio-economic terms, hierarchies are socialist and edge organizations are marketplaces. Edge organizations are organizations where everyone is empowered by information and has the freedom to do what makes sense. They are organizations that embody a *power to the edge* approach to command and control.

NOTES

1   For DoD, this supporting infostructure is called the *Global Information Grid* and its supporting policies, protocols, procedures, and architectures are discussed later in this book.

2   Gove, Philip Babcock, ed. *Webster's Third New International Dictionary.* Springfield, MA: Merriam-Webster, Inc. January 2002.

3   Petress, Ken. *Power: Definition, Typology, Description, Examples, and Implications.* http://www.umpi.maine.edu/~petress/power.pdf. (Feb 1, 2003)

4   *Network Centric Warfare Department of Defense Report to Congress.* July 2001. Executive Summary, p. vii.

5   Hundley, Richard O. *Past Revolutions, Future Transformations: What Can the History of Revolutions in Military Affairs Tell Us About Transforming the U.S. Military?* Santa Monica, CA: RAND. 1999.

6   Suppression of Enemy Air Defenses.

7   Peterson, Rolf O., Amy K. Jacobs, Thomas D. Drummer, L. David Mech, and Douglas W. Smith. "Leadership behavior in relation to dominance and reproductive status in gray wolves, Canis lupus." *Canadian Journal of Zoology.*

Ottawa, CAN: NRC Research Press. Aug 2002.
http://canis.tamu.edu/wfscCourses/Examples/RefWolf.html. (May 1, 2003)

8   Mission Capability Package (MCP). *Network Centric Warfare Department of Defense Report to Congress.* 2001.
http://www.c3i.osd.mil/NCW/ncw_sense.pdf. pp. 18-19. (Feb 1, 2003)

9   The nature of the interactions that take place is a key component of the conceptual framework developed in a research initiative jointly sponsored by ASD(NII) and the Office of Force Transformation. It is discussed more fully in Chapter 3.

10   The discussion that follows is adapted from:
Leavitt, Harold J. and Homa Bahrami, *Managerial Psychology: Managing Behavior in Organizations.* Chicago, IL: University of Chicago Press. 1988. pp. 208-216.

11   Press Release by U.S. Senator Chuck Schumer. *Poor Communication Between FBI and Local Law Enforcement Threatens Public Safety.* Dec 11, 2001.
http://www.senate.gov/~schumer/SchumerWebsite/pressroom/press_releases/PR00758.html. (Apr 1, 2003)
U.S. Conference of Mayors. *Status Report on Federal-Local Homeland Security Partnership.* September 2, 2002.
http://www.usmayors.org/USCM/news/press_releases/documents/911_090902.asp. (Apr 1, 2003)

12   Bakel, Rogier van. "Origin's Original." *Wired.* New York, NY: Wired News. Issue 4.11. 1996.

Chapter 10

Power to the Edge

All of the necessary ingredients for a discussion of the concept of *power to the edge* have now been introduced. These include: the essence of command and control; the Industrial Age approach to command and control; the capabilities that define the Information Age; the capabilities that Information Age militaries need to have; and the meanings of *power* and the *edge* in the context of military operations.

Power to the edge represents a new way of thinking, a new approach to getting things done. This new approach can be applied to designing organizations and developing approaches to command and control, and can be instantiated in systems architectures. *Power to the edge* is also an organizing principle that can be used to allocate responsibilities and resources in military missions. Understanding *power to the edge* enables one to distinguish between desirable and undesirable behaviors. This, in turn, provides the basis for education and training. When fully applied to the design and management of a mission capability package, the result will be an instantiation of the tenets of NCW. When applied to an organization and its processes, the result will be an edge organization. When fully applied to systems architectures, the result will be an edge infostructure that has the characteristics of DoD's future Global Information Grid.

The organizational C2, doctrinal, training, and architectural instantiations of *power to the edge* are all necessary to achieve the goal of bringing all available information and assets to bear. Each of these components of a mission capability package needs to be reconceptualized from a *power to the edge* perspective so that they can be coevolved to create synergistic mission capability packages that can realize the enormous potential power of an Information Age military. It does not end with new MCPs. On the contrary, they are just the beginning, the creation of an organization that can achieve agility and remain agile. The goal is not to be able to perform well in a particular mission in a particular situation, but to create an organization that is agile.

Power to the edge involves a fundamental change in culture. Culture is all about value propositions and behaviors–about who and what is valued, and what constitutes appropriate behavior. *Power to the edge* involves changes in the way we think about the value of entities and desirable behaviors and interactions. Ultimately, this involves a redefinition of self and the relationship between self and others, and self and the enterprise. Thus, in order to move power to the edge, we need to do more than redraw an organization chart; we also need to change what is valued and the way individuals think and behave. We need to rethink the way the enterprise is motivated and led. We need to revamp processes and the systems that support these processes. We need to reeducate and retrain.

The sections that follow address, in turn, what characteristics in organization, command, control, processes, systems, education, and training are needed to move power to the edge.

EDGE ORGANIZATIONS

There are, of course, many structural forms that organizations can adopt. Each surviving organization has a structure that is well adapted to its particular set of purposes and conditions, defined by the characteristics of its objectives, the nature of the tasks that it needs to perform, and its environment. Traditional military organizations are hierarchical structures that are well adapted to take on symmetrical adversaries on a linear battlefield. Historically, military organizations have found it difficult to deal with asymmetrical adversaries such as guerillas or terrorists. They have also found it difficult to operate in a nonlinear battlespace.

As discussed earlier, military organizations have adapted to their circumstances and environments by developing different approaches to command and control. These adaptations, while resulting in quite different power topologies, have nevertheless been limited by the available technology, existing cultures, and hierarchical structures.

One way to define an organization's structure is to specify the nature of the interactions[1] that take place among its members.[2] The interactions between and among members of the organization form the links in a network and collectively define its

topology. Networks (nodes and links) with different characteristics correspond to different organizational structures that
inherit the characteristics of the network. That is, there is a
mapping from a communications network of members to
organizational structure and to its inherent characteristics.
How organizations function is affected by the connections that
exist or do not exist and how these connections are utilized.
Figure 24 depicts four different ways that a five-node network
can be "wired." Network topologies 1 and 2 have a "boss."
From left to right, Network 1 represents a flattened hierarchy
while Network 2 represents a traditional hierarchy. Network 3
represents a robustly networked organization. Network 4 represents a circle.

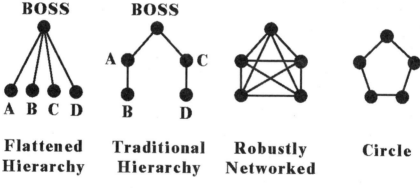

Figure 24. Four Network Topologies

Organizational Structure and Power

The appropriateness of a given organizational structure (topology of interactions) depends upon the nature of the load
placed on an organization. To understand how structure,
load, and performance are related, we can begin by examining
the capability of an organization to perform a key task that all
organizations need to accomplish–the task of sensemaking.

The first step is to be able to see how structure affects the ability of an organization to accomplish a single, rather simple repetitive task. The second step is to change the task and see how well the organization learns (adapts). This introduces one dimension of complexity. After we examine organizational structure and performance with a single task, we will extend the discussion to organizations that need to accomplish many tasks simultaneously in a dynamic environment.

The effect of structure on the ability of an organization to make sense of a situation (also referred to by some as *problem solving*) has been studied often.[3] One particularly interesting set of experiments was conducted by Leavitt and Bahrami.[4] They sought to find out the relative problem solving abilities of groups of individuals organized in two of the ways depicted in Figure 24, a traditional hierarchy and a circle. The specific question they posed was "How does the communication network affect both the efficiency of the performance and the morale of members?" The experiment compared a traditional hierarchy with a circle structure. Each organization was given the same puzzle that required some piece of information from each member. Thus, both how information was shared and how decisions were made were hypothesized to be critical to performance.

Leavitt and Bahrami reported the following results:

- Speed: The traditional hierarchy was the fastest.

- Morale: Members in the circle had, on average, better morale. Only one person in the traditional hierarchy had high morale, the boss.

- Leadership: In the circle, different members took the lead at different times.

- Learning: The circle learns faster.

While these results are clearly open to interpretation, it seems clear that the traditional hierarchy proved best suited for stable (and simple) situations, given that morale does not eventually become a problem. The circle organization proved best for a more complex (dynamic) situation where learning is involved. What is interesting to note is that given these two network forms, one has to make a choice between performance and durability (longevity) and between speed and adaptability.

FIXED V. EMERGENT LEADERSHIP

This experiment compared an organization where there was a designated boss (the hierarchy) to one where no one was selected to be the boss (the circle). Earlier work by Leavitt[5] involved organizations connected in ways identical to the flattened and traditional hierarchy but with no designated individual as the boss. He hypothesized that "centrality" was related to behavior, that a centrally-located individual, one with the most access to information (links to others), would emerge as a leader. The results of this experiment supported this line of reasoning.

This is a very important conclusion for NCW. It explains why it is possible for a network-centric organization to self-synchronize rather than be aimless or incoherent, as some have feared. The reason is that the leader for a particular task at a particular time (and place) emerges. Exactly who "takes charge" will differ as a function of the characteristics of the individuals and the situation. When the most well suited or situated individual or organization is in charge, then the organization can be said to be a meritocracy.

This seems to be a property that is more likely to be associated with nonhierarchical forms of organizations. On the other hand, there is evidence that hierarchies ossify. As hierarchies age, they tend to acquire the characteristics associated with bureaucracy, including inflexibility, inefficiency, and fragility.[6]

It also explains why the empowerment of the edge is the key to handling large numbers of simultaneous tasks in a dynamic environment. This is because empowered individuals and organizations that constitute an edge organization have a greater "bandwidth" for action than their unempowered counterparts in traditional hierarchies.

However, the experimental findings that compared the traditional hierarchy with the circle seemed to imply that we need to choose between performance and durability on the one hand and longevity on the other, or between speed and adaptability.

Fortunately, we do not have to make these choices. Information Age technologies now allow us to create a robustly networked organization that can give everyone a prime (central) location on the network. This makes it possible to dynamically adjust the roles and responsibilities of members in response to the task(s) at hand, the characteristics of the operating environment(s), the skills and experiences of the individuals, and the means at their disposal. This both improves morale (by virtue of empowering individuals at the edge of an organization) and facilitates adaptability. The concept of adaptability (changes in organization and work processes) is a crucial element of agility. However, it directly contradicts Industrial Age solutions of complexity, decomposition, deconfliction, specialization, and optimization.

In any significant military operation, there will be many tasks that need to be accomplished under the press of time. The success of these operations will depend, in large measure, on both (1) how well each of these tasks is done and (2) how well these tasks are synchronized. The timeliness requirement makes it imperative that an organization be capable of multitasking (doing several things in parallel). To be successful, the individuals and organizations engaged in each task need access to the appropriate means, including information about what else is affecting the aspects of the environment that are related to their task. They also need access to the appropriate expertise, tools, supplies, etc.

However, a network topology alone will not achieve the desired result; it does not create the conditions necessary to achieve productive self-synchronization. To complete the package, a suitable approach to command and control must be developed to leverage the capabilities provided by a robustly connected network topology.

AN EDGE INFOSTRUCTURE

Information is the lifeblood of Information Age organizations. Information-related policies and architectures define the topology and determine the capabilities of an organization to distribute this vital resource. DoD is making progress on the deployment of an Information Age infostructure, referred to as the Global Information Grid, conceived with *power to the edge* principles and accompanied by policies that reflect a *power to the edge* philosophy.[7] The GIG will provide a set of secure information and telecommunication services that will enhance sensemaking[8] and support collaboration, both of which are essential to promote a high level of shared awareness and to create the conditions needed for effective self-synchronization.

The GIG itself will increasingly become an adaptive entity that integrates communication and computer systems into a secure, seamless infostructure, one that provides access to a variety of information sources and information management resources. GIG components will share status information with each other, enabling the GIG to dynamically respond to user requirements and adapt to stresses imposed on the network, including those that may be caused by an adversary attack. These characteristics of the GIG also enable it to change its scale as necessary to support force structure(s) of arbitrary size, and/or to incorporate new processing, networking, and communication technologies as they are needed. Thus, the GIG is a dynamically scaleable environment with a great deal of agility. Figure 25 provides a conceptual view of the GIG.

Components of the GIG

The GIG will be a distributed environment that includes all types of computers situated at locations all around the world as appropriate with varying needs for power, environment, and space. This distributed environment will be integrated via a transport layer that enables these processors to exchange information, dynamically share workloads, and cooperatively process information on behalf of (and transparent to) users. The GIG will make information and related services available to any and all connected entities (nodes) that are "net ready." Competitive market mechanisms will ensure that users have

Entities

– Sources and users of information
– Diversity of information needs
  - Type, quantity, timeliness
  - Change as a function of mission & situation

Integrated Information infrastructure (III) functional decomposition

– Layered concept. Each layer:
  - Provides services to layer above
  - Receives services from layers below
  - Dynamically adapts to meet information needs of entities
  - Tightly coupled to each other to permit adaptation as an integrated system

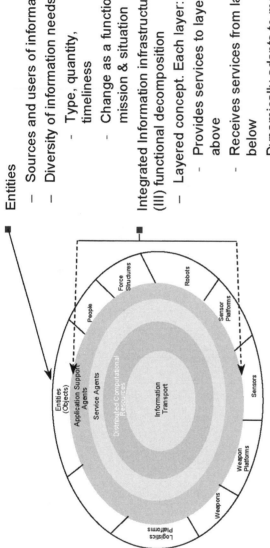

Force Structures
People
Robots
Sensor Platforms
Entities (Objects)
Application Support Agents
Service Agents
Distributed Computational Resources
Information Transport
Sensors
Weapon Platforms
Weapons
Logistics Platforms

■ Agents = a software entity that is autonomous, is goal directed, is migratory, is able to create other entities and provides a service or function on behalf of its owner

Figure 25. The Global Information Grid–Conceptual View

access to the information and services that they want when, where, and how they want it.

GIG Data Policy and Practices

As explained earlier, to promote the necessary widespread sharing of information, DoD policy envisions that users will post all of the information they collect or produce so that it can be immediately available to those who need it. To make this information understandable across the enterprise, information that is posted must be accompanied by metadata–data that briefly describe and classify the information to which it is appended. This will allow users to quickly identify what would be most valuable for their particular needs. By requiring a minimum set of metadata for all posted information, a robust search process is enabled across the enterprise and we will be better able to bring all of our information to bear.

The minimum set of required metadata includes parameters such as the source of the information, a description of the information, its intended use, the pedigree, and the security classification level.

GIG Net-Centric Enterprise Services

Figure 26 depicts GIG User Services. Metadata posting, collection, and management capabilities will be deployed as part of the infrastructure's Net-Centric Enterprise Services (NCES). Thus, the GIG will provide the following services:

- Facilities to permit advertising of the availability of information through original and value-added sources;

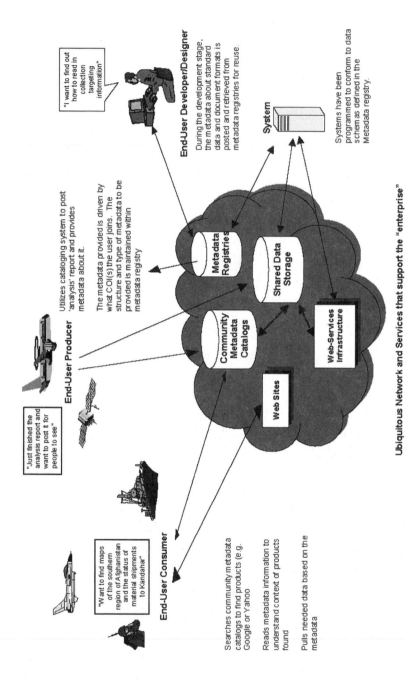

Figure 26. GIG User Services

- Discovery mechanisms to locate and identify information to support user tasks; and

- Mediation services to translate, fuse, and aggregate data elements into information that addresses the users' current needs. These information services will include flexible access control mechanisms that facilitate visibility and availability (while hiding information where there is an explicit need for security beyond that afforded by the network).

Furthermore, the user will be able to search catalogs of services available on the GIG. These catalogs will contain information that describes the capabilities of the service, the necessary inputs to use the service and the outputs of the service. For example, a producer community can offer a service that allows a user to query a database, such as the Military Intelligence Database (MIDB), for specific information rather than requiring a user to develop his/her own application to accomplish that task.

GIG Agents

The GIG "information marketplace" will have agent-based services available that can tailor information to meet the needs of diverse users ranging from individuals to teams and organizations, and to sensors and/or weapons systems. These software agents will be autonomous, goal directed, and migratory. These agents, under the general control of a user or set of users, will also be able to create other software entities. These agents will use the metadata and NCES to proactively pull and appropriately package information for users. They will perform such functions as fusing and filtering information, and automatically deliver the right information to the right user at the right time.[9] Agents are proactive in the sense that they can be designed to be aware of the user's situation and information needs, and can provide information relevant to those needs without a specific user request. Figure 27 provides a conceptual rendering of these agents.

Agents greatly multiply the personnel resources available to combat units by gathering and transforming raw data into actionable information to support unit operations, just as unit members would do themselves were the software agents not provided. Warfighters and those that support them will therefore be freed from routine chores and will be able to devote more attention to operations.

The GIG Powering the Edge

Because computing resources are distributed throughout the infostructure, the GIG will adjust the amount of processing resources available to any given force (edge) entity. The edge entities' processor need only be net-ready, meaning connected to the GIG, provide an adequate interface to the user entity, and enable the acquisition and presentation of information to the user. Thus, for example, a dismounted infantry-person's information resources could be a thin client dedicated to supporting a rich human-computer interface (with voice recognition, heads-up display, speech synthesis, and communications) and would not have to have its scarce computing capacity tied up with providing other information-related services. General computing resources to support an edge user could reside elsewhere on the net.

Components of the GIG

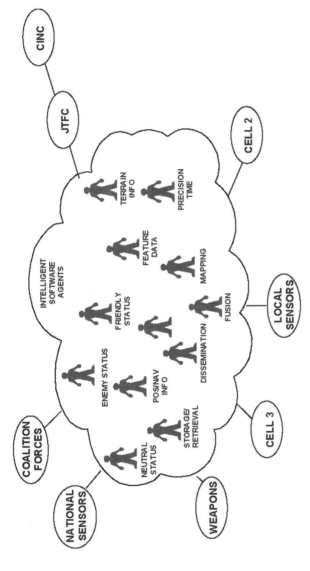

Figure 27. GIG Software Agents

- Intelligent Software Agents:
  - Relieve users of information management functions
  - Provide data fusion, information storage, retrieval and dissemination
  - Tailor information at the right time, to the combat cells needing it
  - Allow users to request information in mission specific terms
  - Provide geospatial and time information services

GIG's Internet Protocol-Based Transport Layer

The GIG will include multimode data transport media including land-line, radio, and space-based elements. All of these media will be integrated into a ubiquitous, store-and-forward Internet that dynamically routes information from source(s) to destination(s), transparently to the user. The GIG transport layer (Figure 28) will be self-managed, be adaptive to node or link failure, and provide services to its users based on quality-of-service (QoS) requests. These services include bandwidth, latency, reliability, precedence, distribution mechanisms (point-to-point, point-to-multipoint), and the like. Dynamic, multihop, beyond line-of-sight services will be provided through network routing functions supported in routers, the Joint Tactical Radio System (JTRS), and satellites. Automatic routing and relaying will take place on platforms using JTRS running the wideband network waveform (WNW). The WNW will support network services based on mobile ad hoc networking technologies pioneered in the Defense Advance Research Projects Agency's (DARPA) Packet Radio Program. These technologies will permit all JTRS-equipped aircraft (manned or unmanned), all JTRS-equipped ground platforms, and other platforms to automatically become members of JTRS networks and provide adaptive, self-managed communication relaying services.[10]

To the maximum extent feasible, the transport layer will take advantage of commercial technology and networks by utilizing open-systems standards and protocols and minimizing the use of service or function-unique hardware and software. The Internet Protocol (IP) will be the common standard that will facilitate interoperability amongst the multimode transport media. These media will become IP aware to allow data to

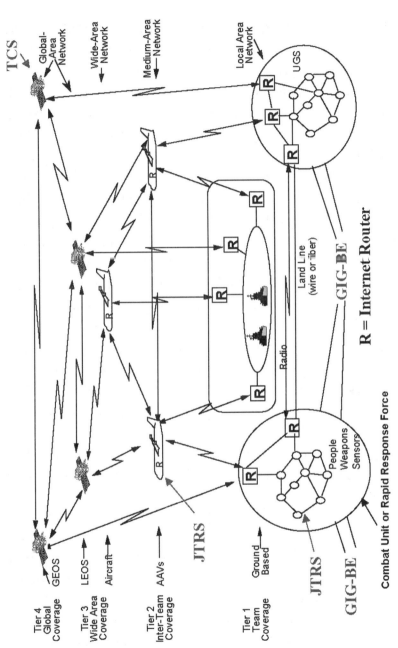

Figure 28. GIG Transport Layer

move seamlessly between all entities on the GIG. For applications where military-unique capabilities (such as anti-jam, low probability of intercept, spread-spectrum waveforms and the like) are required, military products will be developed or adapted to interface with the overall IP-based architecture.

Security for the GIG merits special discussion. The exploitation of commercial protocols and standards provides the technology base necessary. Because portions of the infostructure will incorporate commercial network technology, and much of it will be based on commercial information management technology, security must be an integral design consideration throughout development. Further, because the GIG will necessarily incorporate commercial telecommunication systems, these systems must be carefully evaluated to balance the benefit versus the risk for each such incorporation. For the transport layer of the GIG, careful attention to Information Operations (IO) is essential. DoD is working with industry to ensure that the space-based segment of the GIG is resilient and can withstand IO attacks. For example, protection of the control and signaling channels for the space nodes is critical. Similarly, DoD will continue to be the focal point for developing low probability of intercept (LPI) and low probability detection (LPD) waveforms for the networked, primarily ground-based communication networks described previously. The software-programmable radios (JTRS) provide the flexibility needed to implement an adaptable, self-managed transport capability, as envisioned of the GIG. This same flexibility provides an opportunity to enhance information assurance (IA) services. For example, the network-level protocols for these radios could make every node look the same (in a traffic analysis) as any other node, thereby limiting an adversary's ability to identify and target high-value, force-structure entities such as command and control centers. Similarly, the network-level protocols could, if the system detects an attack, change its waveforms in such a manner that the radio emissions appear to be those of an adversary's unit, or change it to cause a radio node to appear to be a radar site. Network protocols and algorithms could achieve radio-network-based cover, concealment, and deception (CCD) in ways never before conceived.

Commercial market forces are expected to continue to aggressively motivate the private sector to provide increased security for the Web. Specifically, the growth of electronic commerce has already motivated the development of standards and technology for conducting secure information transactions. Examples of these standards and technologies are Internet Protocol Security (IPSec), Secure Socket Layer (SSL), public key infrastructure (PKI) and key distribution mechanisms, strong encryption algorithms, intrusion detection systems, and inexpensive biometric systems (fingerprint readers and retinal scanners). These standards provide for information authentication, nonrepudiation, and secure transport.[11]

Furthermore, the private sector is starting to address the issues of security for mobile code, the countering of denial of service attacks, and the insider threat. As noted earlier, examples of mobile code are Java applets that are downloaded onto a user's machine and executed locally, or migratory intelligent software agents as described previously. Several approaches have been identified for securing such code (e.g., sandboxing, code-signing, firewalling, and proof-carrying code); however, these approaches have yet to be implemented, tested, and standardized.

Appropriate security for a distributed infostructure must be realized through the development of a comprehensive security architecture, security policy, training, and testing. Leveraging commercial security technology and techniques, the architecture must provide flexible, dynamic, adaptive, and rapidly reconfigurable security in support of the software agents at work in the infrastructure, combining security technology available today from the private sector that, when combined with DoD developed network encryption systems, can provide acceptable security for the GIG. Employing a defense-in-depth architecture, leveraging IP encryption, PKI, firewalls, application gateways, and certificate-based selective access to information bases should provide protection for the GIG if appropriate security policies, system configuration and management processes, and security accountability are enforced by the Department of Defense.

EDGE APPLICATIONS

Earlier we noted that NCW *power to the edge* requires a new approach to interoperability, one that focuses on data rather than on applications. The idea is that everyone (with proper permissions) can access the data that they need by using applications that suit their purposes, and do not need to rely on "one size fits all" applications developed by a surrogate user. They will develop greater capabilities more rapidly–capabilities that are better tailored, better understood, and easier to use and modify. The proviso is that these edge applications must be able to post the data that they produce in a form that others can use (e.g., adhere to metadata standards and processes).

Many say that this is good in theory, but that it takes "professional" organizations to develop applications. Others have argued that COTS products are now (or soon will become) powerful enough for relatively unsophisticated users (who are not software developers) to create powerful applications. The Navy Special Warfare Mission Support Center has provided us with a proof of concept. Using Microsoft NetMeeting and other commercial products, they were able to support the information needs of multiple SEAL teams in real time during operations in both Afghanistan and Iraq.[12] They provided a "value-added" information service at the edge with existing personnel and COTS software.

As we move further into the 21st century, we can expect that edge personnel will have increasingly proficient computer literacy and that more powerful COTS tools will be available. We need to encourage these efforts and learn how to (1) ensure the data interoperability that we need, (2) promulgate good ideas and COTS applications, and (3) see how our systems professionals can better support the edge.

NOTES

1 The nature of the interactions that take place is a key component of the conceptual framework developed in a research initiative jointly sponsored by ASD(NII) and the Office of Force Transformation. It is discussed more fully in Chapter 3.

2 The discussion that follows is adapted from Leavitt, Harold J. and Homa Bahrami. *Managerial Psychology: Managing Behavior in Organizations.* Chicago, Il: University of Chicago Press. 1988. pp. 208-216.

3 Bigley, G.A. and Roberts, K.H. "The Incident Command System: High Reliability Organizing for Complex and Volatile Task Environments." *Academy of Management Journal.* Vol 44, Number 6. 2001. pp. 1281-1300. Weick, K.E. & Sutcliffe, K.M. "Managing the Unexpected: Assuring High

Performance in an Age of Complexity." San Francisco, CA: Jossey-Wiley. 2001.

4   Leavitt, *Managerial Psychology.*

5   Leavitt, Harold J. "Some Effect of Certain Communication Patterns on Group Performance" *Journal of Abnormal and Social Psychology.* 1951. pp. 38-50.

6   Cabral, Ana Maria Rezende. "Participatory Management." Anthony Vaughn. *International Reader in the Management of Library, Information and Archive Services.* Paris, FR: UNESCO. 1986. Section 5.11.

7   This section is based on discussions with and a paper entitled "The Vision for a Global Information Grid (GIG)" by Michael Frankel, currently the Deputy Assistant Secretary of Defense for Programs in the Office of the Assistant Secretary of Defense (NII).

8   Sensemaking is defined as the process of creating situation awareness in situations of uncertainty.
Leedom, Dennis K. "Sensemaking Experts Panel Meeting Final Report." Vienna, VA: EBR, Inc. June 2002.
Leedom, Dennis K. "Sensemaking Symposium Final Report." Vienna, VA: EBR, Inc. October 2001.

9   This is clearly overstated. But to the extent that users know what they need and to the extent the information is available this seemingly bold statement can be turned into a reality.

10 Capstone Requirements Document (CRD). *Global Information Grid (GIG).* March 28, 2001.
http://www.dfas.mil/technology/pal/regs/gigcrdflaglevelreview.pdf. (Apr 1, 2003)

11 Rogers, Amy. "Maximum Security." *Computer Reseller News.* Manhasset. Sep 20, 1999.
Rollender, Matt. "SSL: The secret handshake of the 'Net." *Network World.* Framingham. Feb 3, 2003.
Borck, James. "Building Your Site from Scratch." *InfoWorld.* Framingham. Oct 4, 1999.

12 Ackerman, Robert K. "Special Forces Become Network-Centric." *SIGNAL Magazine.* Fairfax, VA: AFCEA. March 2003.
http://us.net/signal/Archive/March03/special-march.html. (May 1, 2003)

Chapter 11

Command... Control...in the Information Age

Traditional command and control principles and practices have evolved over time in response to the nature of the threat, the nature of the forces, and the information technologies available. However, evolutionary processes are relatively slow. Darwin's "survival of the fittest" depends upon natural selection where the offspring of survivors have better adapted features than those that do not survive. Extinction occurs when changes in the environment are too rapid. Revolutions in Military Affairs (RMAs) have occurred, but many were slow to develop, developing long after the availability of the enabling capability. The delays for the most part were due to cultural barriers.

Transformation is an effort to accelerate adaptation to maintain competitive advantage. DoD's commitment to transformation is an explicit recognition that something needs to change sooner rather than later. It means changing even if you currently are (or think you are) the best. This is very difficult for many to accept, and as a result there is less than universal commitment to the kind of transformation described in *Information Age Transformation*.[1] NCW is identified in this book as a central focus of transformation efforts. This is because it is understood that existing command and control concepts and processes are no longer adequate to accommodate current and emerging threats and significant changes in the security environment, and that significant advances in information technologies and their employment offer us the opportunity to rethink command and control. To become an Information Age organization, a military organization will need to fundamentally change their approach to command and control. This means that they will need to change the way they think about information and its dissemination, and about accomplishing tasks, organizing, and training. This also means that they need to explore new interactions among individuals and organizations and develop new processes.

This chapter describes the nature of command and control in the Information Age, an approach based upon the tenets of NCW and the principles of *power to the edge*. This new approach to command...control...involves separating the two components of C2 into (1) the nature of command in the Information Age and (2) how control will be achieved.

COMMAND IN THE INFORMATION AGE

It is hard to separate the wheat from the chaff of command by reading military history literature from the "great leader" or "genius" school.[2] The emphasis on a single, heroic commander who is all things to all people is pervasive. In fact, much of the literature on command would have one believe that the organization exists primarily to serve the commander. To some extent, this is reflected in Industrial Age C2 systems and processes, particularly by the largely vertical one-way flows of information and the emphasis on supporting the decisionmaker (emphasis on the singular). This view of command could be characterized as *power to the center.* Systemic faults found in organizations of this type include the mismatches that frequently occur between responsibility and authority and the great disparities that often exist among levels of awareness that lead to a lack of effectiveness and agility. Many successful individuals in senior positions in all kinds of organizations understand differently. They understand that the organization does not exist to serve them, but rather that they exist to serve the organization, to work with others to help to create the conditions necessary for success.

Command in the Information Age is ultimately not the sole responsibility of any single individual. It is a shared and distributed responsibility. Does this mean that no one is in charge? This question is at the heart of the matter. The simple truth is that there are in fact many instances where no one is in charge of an enterprise or endeavor today. Who, for example, is in charge of the U.N. Security Council? Who is in charge of a coalition of the willing? Is the leader of the government of a nation in charge of that nation? What, in fact, does *in charge* mean? Is being in charge merely a fixing of responsibility and/

or a capability to give an order, as stated in the first two definitions listed in the dictionary, "to impose a duty, responsibility, or obligation on" and "to set or ask"?[3]

Some would say that being in charge pertains to the degree of influence that one has. That is, if you are *in control*, then you are *in charge*. Certainly there is no value derived from the case when there can be command with little or no influence (no control), unless the objective is to have someone to blame. Thus, merely putting someone in charge does not result in either effective command or control.

While there still may be situations in which it is possible for one person to successfully discharge all of the responsibilities of command, virtually all significant military operations undertaken in the 21st century will require that the function of command be accomplished in a distributed and collaborative fashion. This is obviously the case in coalition operations, but it has also been the case in U.S.-only military organizations. For example, in Somalia[4] responsibilities for forces in theater were divided between the CJTF and the CINC, with the CJTF not having command over certain Special Forces.[5] Situations in which no one person has full authority over forces are common. There are terms used to describe various degrees of command including combatant command (COCOM), operational command (OPCOM), and tactical command (TACOM).[6] With the increasing importance of information in operations, the lines of responsibility for task information collection, analysis, and distribution will become as important as command arrangements. Intelligence organizations exist both within and outside of the military, even outside of the U.S. Government. All of these intelligence organizations may develop information that is critical to a mission, but it is inconceivable that someone will be in command of all these information assets. Thus, individuals at all levels in many organizations will need to be able to work with others both within their organization and with others in a variety of other organizations to collectively exercise the functions of command.

The definition of command has often been linked to the position of a commander, as in "whatever a commander does is command."[7] In missions of any significance there are, of course, many commanders, each with an area of responsibility. Except in the case when a strict hierarchy exists, no one commander is in charge of all military forces. For the discussion of command in the Information Age, we will assume that, as is the case in virtually all recent operations, there is no single person in charge and we will separate the commander(s) from the function of command because commanders perform a variety of functions.[8]

Command[9] in the Information Age involves creating the conditions for success, including the selection of a vision and associated goals, the development of objectives, the setting of priorities, the allocation of resources, and the establishment of constraints. Taken together, these (1) define the problem to be addressed or the mission to be accomplished and constitute *command intent* and (2) scope the solution. Implicit in this formulation is the recognition of a need to modify or change intent and/or the solution approach as the need arises. In a coalition environment, the maintenance of the coalition (shared intent) is a very important element of command.

To ascertain the quality of command in a given situation, four attributes need to be addressed: (1) the quality of the formulation of intent, (2) the degree to which the intent is understood (correct and shared), (3) the quality of the solution approach, and (4) the responsiveness related to making appropriate changes.

This formulation of command in the Information Age is the instantiation of *power to the edge* in the domain of command and control. To be fully effective, the principles of *power to the edge* also need to be applied to all of the other aspects of the enterprise.

CONTROL IN THE INFORMATION AGE

It has been said that while command is an art, control is a science.[10] This oversimplification is nevertheless a useful distinction. In the Industrial Age, the science of control was Control Theory.[11] In the Information Age, the science of control has its basis in the new sciences of complexity. *Coping with the Bounds*[12] discusses the need to understand the nonlinearity inherent in military operations. *Effects Based Operations*[13] speaks to the need to understand the effects of actions in the military domain upon other domains, and vice versa. This increase in the dimensionality of mission effectiveness adds to complexity and highlights the importance of developing an understanding of the nature of complex adaptive systems.

Control Theory requires both prediction and the existence of an adequate set of levers of control. We are all familiar with the inability of economists to predict economic performance and the lackluster track record of various attempts to control the economy. All of us are familiar with efforts by meteorologists to forecast just one day into the future. Thus, prediction is very difficult even for normal, day-to-day events (even if there is no intelligent adversary working against you). Having effective, centrally managed levers that can control or even predictably influence a complex, adaptive system is far from guaranteed.

As though it were not difficult enough, many Industrial Age command and control processes seek to optimize. In reality, optimization is not even an option. A more realistic control objective than the pursuit of optimality is to keep a situation within bounds while accomplishing an objective. For some missions (e.g., peacekeeping), keeping the situation within bounds *is* the mission. Naturally, how tightly the bounds are set will determine the degree of challenge. For example, the challenge in taking a military objective within a certain amount of time, with limited collateral damage and with a limited number of casualties, depends (all things being equal) on how much time, how much collateral damage, and how many casualties are "acceptable."

Our objective in controlling classified or sensitive information has also undergone a change in recent years from strictly limiting access to information in an attempt to prevent compromise to a risk management approach. In other words, our objective has become to keep a situation within bounds, rather than seeking an optimal solution. This notion of managing the risk associated with a situation (keeping a situation within bounds) is the appropriate control objective for the Information Age.

In addition to changing the nature of the control objective, we also need to shift our approach to achieving it. How can we best accomplish our control objective(s)? In the Industrial Age, our approach to control was to establish a plan and set up a separate quality control process that mirrored the hierarchy of the organization. The job of this control process was to observe what was happening and intervene when things were not going according to plan. Thus control was essentially centralized.

The ability to control the situation (to be *in control*) using this centralized approach depends upon the ability to develop a quality plan, one that can survive for a reasonable amount of time. This means that the plan needs to remain effective for at least as long as it takes to begin to disseminate and implement the plan, determine its effectiveness, and replan if need be. Increasingly, this is exceedingly difficult or simply not possible.[14] The failings of centralized control are intertwined with the failings of hierarchies to marshal available information and assets and be responsive to changes in the environment. While this Industrial Age approach to control goes hand in hand with traditional hierarchical military organizations, edge organizations require a different approach to control.

In the Information Age, control needs to be thought about and approached differently. Control is not something that can be imposed on a complex adaptive system, particularly when there are many independent actors. Control, that is, ensuring that behavior stays within or moving to within acceptable bounds, can only be achieved indirectly. The most promising approach involves establishing, to the extent possible, a set of initial conditions that will *result*[15] in the desired behavior. In other words, control is not achieved by imposing a parallel process, but rather emerges from influencing the behaviors of independent agents. Instead of being *in control*, the enterprise creates the conditions that are likely to give rise to the behaviors that are desired.

Emergent behavior is not new, but it has only recently been identified and studied.[16] The magic of NCW, the leap from shared awareness to self-synchronization, is a form of emergent behavior. NCW works because it has identified, in general terms, the initial conditions that need to exist in order to achieve effective self-synchronization.

Measuring control in the Information Age is no different because the desired result is the same. However, the independent variables to track it (collect data about and analyze) will be different. These independent variables will include the initial conditions that are hypothesized to influence behaviors.

The ideas expressed here (Command...Control...in the Information Age) have sparked concerns about accountability. Some think that if "no one is in charge" then no one will be accountable. Nothing is further from the truth. If anything, it will be easier to hold individuals accountable for their actions because there will be a greater shared understanding of the situation than ever before. This includes an understanding of command intent, assigned resources, rules of engagement, and the status of one's assets.

The individuals and organizations that contribute to the exercise of the command function are clearly responsible for creating the initial conditions from which desirable behaviors will emerge. They will be provided, more than ever before, with access to information and expertise in real time. While it is unfair and unproductive to hold people accountable for things they cannot control (something that happens all too frequently today), it is important to hold people accountable for doing their jobs to the best of their abilities. These individuals and organizations are responsible for monitoring the situation, making adjustments to the initial conditions when appropriate, and making certain that others share their perceptions. This should not be taken as an excuse to micromanage, an inappropriate and counterproductive behavior that in and of itself constitutes a failure to properly discharge one's responsibilities. In the Information Age, command will be exercised in ways that are not unfamiliar—establishing congruent command intent across the enterprise, allocating resources dynamically, and establishing rules of engagement.

New norms of behavior (needed to provide a standard for accountability) are in the process of being established. It will take time, a great deal of experimentation, and experience for norms to be developed, accepted, widely understood, and universally applied. The lack of established standards is no reason not to change the way that we accomplish the function of command and promote desirable behaviors. We need to remember that existing C2 approaches and processes, however well understood, are not well suited to meet emerging security challenges and have accountability problems of their own. However, accountability problems experienced during a transition to Information Age command...control...can be minimized if common sense is used. This means that a standard of reasonableness needs to be applied, rather than an inflexible standard.

NOTES

1   Alberts, *Information Age Transformation.*

2   Meyer and Davis argue that "we have greater understanding of the means of adaptation than ever before, so that we can articulate these management rules more precisely, implement them more systematically, and rely less on the intuition of a few gifted leaders."
Meyer, Christopher, and Stan Davis. "Embracing Evolution: Business from the Bottom Up." *Perspectives on Business Innovation.* Issue 9. Cambridge, MA: Center for Business Innovation. Spring 2003.
http://www.cbi.cgey.com/journal/index.html. (Apr 1, 2003)

3   *The American Heritage® Dictionary of the English Language,* Fourth Edition. Boston, MA: Houghton Mifflin Company. 2000.

4   Allard, Kenneth. *Somalia Operations: Lessons Learned*. Washington, DC: CCRP
    Publication Series. January 1995. p. 26.
    Joint Military Operations Historical Collection. July 15, 1997. p. VI-1.
    http://www.dtic.mil/doctrine/jel/history/hist.pdf. (Apr 1, 2003)

5   Alberts, *Command Arrangements*.

6   Alberts, *Command Arrangements*. p. 9.

7   DoD defines command as "the authority that a commander in the Military
    Service lawfully exercises over subordinates by virtue of rank or
    assignment." Therefore, command is a function of the actions of a
    commander. Department of Defense Dictionary of Military and Associated
    Terms. Joint Pubs. 1-02.
    http://www.dtic.mil/doctrine/jel/doddict/. (Apr 1, 2003)

8   In the future, commanders will continue to perform a variety of functions,
    but perhaps not all of the functions that they perform today, and perhaps
    some new ones.

9   It should be noted that this discussion of command does not include the
    functions of leadership, functions that may be performed by some of but not
    necessarily the same individuals engaged in command.

10 Alberts, *Command Arrangements*. pp. 7-9. Figure 1.

11 Van Trees, Harry L. L. *Detection, Estimation, and Modulation Theory, Optimum
    Array Processing*. Wiley, John & Sons, Incorporated. March 2002.

12 Czerwinski, Tom. *Coping with the Bounds: Speculations on Non-Linearity in Military
    Affairs*. Washington, DC: CCRP Publication Series. 1998.

13 Smith, *Effects*.

14 Hayes, Richard E. "Systematic Assessment of C2 Effectiveness and its
    Determinates." Vienna, VA: Evidence Based Research, Inc.
    http://www.dodccrp.org/sm_workshop/pdf/SAC2EID.pdf. (Apr 1, 2003)

15 It has an arbitrarily high probability of doing so.

16 Neck, Christopher P; Manz, Charles C. *From Groupthink to Teamthink: Toward
    the Creation of Constructive Thought Patterns in Self-managing Work Teams*. New
    York, NY: Human Relations. Aug 1994.
    Sinclair, Andrea L. *The Effects of Justice and Cooperation on Team Effectiveness*.
    Thousand Oaks: Small Group Research. Feb 2003.
    Moffat, James. *Complexity Theory and Network Centric Warfare*. Washington, DC:
    CCRP Publication Series. 2003.

Grudin, Jonathan. *Group Dynamics and Ubiquitous Computing Association for Computing Machinery.* New York, NY: Communications of the ACM. Dec 2002.

Harrison, David A, Kenneth H. Price, Joanne H. Gavin, Anna T. Florey. *Time, Teams, and Task Performance: Changing Effects of Surface - and Deep-level Diversity on Group Functioning.* Briarcliff Manor: Academy of Management Journal. Vol 45. Oct 2002.

NOTES

Chapter 12

The Power of "Power to the Edge" Organizations

P ower is an expression of potential. Accomplishment is the realization of power. The concept of *power to the edge* therefore is about the empowerment of the edge of an organization. The reason for moving power to the edge is to make the organization "more powerful." This additional power is related to a corresponding increase in organizational agility. The source of the increased power comes from (1) an improvement in an organization's ability to bring *all* of its information and *all* of its assets to bear, instead of only a fraction of its information and assets, and (2) the ability to recognize and take advantage of fleeting opportunities. In other words, *power to the edge* allows an organization to fully realize its potential power by making the most of the resources it has and the opportunities presented.[1]

If *power to the edge* organizations and architectures are, as we contend, more powerful than current military hierarchies and the systems that support them, then they must be able to accomplish more, in less time, under more adverse conditions, and at lower cost than Industrial Age organizations and architectures. They must also be able to generate more power over a wider mission spectrum and be better able to deal with uncertainty than traditional organizations and architectures.

In military organizations, power is a function of the collective means and opportunity possessed by the individuals in the organization with respect to their ability to accomplish the four minimum essential capabilities required for military operations. These capabilities are:

- The ability to make sense of the situation;

- The ability to work in a coalition environment including nonmilitary (interagency, international organizations and private industry, as well as contractor personnel) partners;

- Possession of the appropriate means to respond; and

- The ability to orchestrate the means to respond in a timely manner.

Thus, the relative ability of an organization to be able to accomplish these minimum essential capabilities in operations that span the mission spectrum is a direct measure of its power.

Three of these four capabilities (first, second, and fourth) are directly related to the ability of an organization to effectively utilize available information. In turn, this ability to exploit information is directly related to organizational topology. Being able to effectively orchestrate means is also directly related to the command and control approach selected by an organization. The third of the minimum essential capabilities, possessing the means to respond, while not directly related to information,[2] is indirectly related in the sense that the cost and effectiveness of means are related to information.[3] Thus power is closely related to the ability of an enterprise to exploit and leverage information.

In this chapter, we identify the basic characteristics of hierarchies and edge organizations and then, by looking at how these characteristics affect their ability to exploit and leverage information, draw inferences regarding their ability to generate power. Simply put, this link between the ability of an organization to use available information to develop shared awareness and then employ shared awareness as a fulcrum to create the conditions necessary for self-synchronization constitutes the Information Age meaning of the phrase "information is power."

HIERARCHIES AND EDGE ORGANIZATIONS

Traditional Hierarchies

A traditional hierarchy has a topology that largely restricts interactions among members of the organization to direct superior/subordinate interactions and whose number of levels is determined by the limits of Industrial Age notions of span of control (maximum of five to seven). Its approach to command

and control is characterized by centralized planning, decomposition of tasks, and control processes that largely rely on deconfliction. Hierarchies spawn stovepipes, which are vertical, tightly coupled component organizations that are optimized for a narrowly focused objective. These stovepipe entities evolve their own cultures and languages. Hence, hierarchies develop into a collection of "tribes." Loyalty is local in nature and internecine (tribal) rivalries are tolerated if not encouraged in the nature of building esprit de corps. A large percentage of the available energy (peoples' time and commitment) is spent internally to establish and maintain "trust," build and maintain loyalty to the "tribe," and establish and employ cross-cutting relationships (often informal) so that the larger organization's goals can be pursued independently of the formal structure.

In these traditional organizations, the systems that support hierarchies are built and controlled by stovepipes, making interoperability difficult to achieve. Furthermore, information flows in hierarchies mirror the hierarchical structure and are largely confined to the stovepipe that originated or collected the information in question. Unless there are considerable pressures to the contrary, hierarchies evolve, not as integrated organizations, but as a federation of individually evolved stovepipes. Even under pressure, information exchanges and collaborations are considered an exception to be accommodated, not as a basic organizing principle.

Edge Organizations

An edge organization encourages appropriate interactions between and among any and all members. Its approach to command and control breaks the traditional C2 mold by uncoupling command from control. Command is involved in setting the initial conditions and providing overall intent. Control is not a function of command but an emergent property that is a function of the initial conditions, the environment, and the adversaries. Loyalty is not to a local entity, but to the overall enterprise.

Edge organizations have the attributes to be agile. This is because agility requires that available information is combined in new ways, that a variety of perspectives are brought to bear, and that assets can be employed differently to meet the needs of a variety of situations. While they are not optimized to accomplish familiar tasks as hierarchies have evolved to do, edge organizations may even be able to develop more innovative solutions to familiar problems over time. This is because hierarchical processes are optimized subject to a set of constraints[4] that do not bound the behavior of edge organizations. Edge organizations are particularly well suited to deal with uncertainty and unfamiliarity because they make more of their relevant knowledge, experience, and expertise available.

Just as Industrial Age militaries relied upon decentralized execution to overcome problems inherent in a relatively slow, ponderous centralized planning process, Industrial Age bureaucracies of all types (including military organizations) relied on informal organizations (for example, "old boy and girl" networks) to overcome the limits imposed by their formal structures and information flows. Unfortunately, these processes lack legitimacy and can only initiate corrective actions when problems arise. The execution of the correction action must be completed with the cooperation of the formal structure, which is often inefficient and unresponsive because its loyalties and reward structures are misaligned. Any effort at reform or revolution must ultimately overcome these barriers.[5]

COMPARISON OF HIERARCHIES V. EDGE ORGANIZATIONS

To first order, hierarchies keep power concentrated in the center (centers in hierarchies have developed powerful stovepipes) while edge organizations move it to the edge.

The ability of any organization to provide the means and opportunities (that constitute power) to those with the responsibilities for dealing with situations and for accomplishing tasks vary as a function of the familiarity of the situation/task at

	Hierarchies	Edge Organizations
Command	By directive	Establishing conditions
Leadership	By position	By competence
Control	By direction	An emergent property
Decisionmaking	Line function	Everyone's job
Information	Hoarded	Shared
Predominant Information Flows	Vertical, coupled with chain of command	Horizontal, independent of chain of command
Information Management	Push	Post - Pull
Sources of Information	Stovepipe monopolies	Eclectic, adaptable marketplaces
Organizational Processes	Prescribed Sequential	Dynamic Concurrent
Individuals at the Edge	Constrained	Empowered

Figure 29. Comparison of Attributes of Hierarchies and Edge Organizations

hand. A look at hierarchies and edge organizations with respect to their ability to handle familiar and unfamiliar tasks is revealing.

If the situation/task is a familiar one, then hierarchies can perform very well (as the research results cited would indicate).[6] The reason is that the organization and processes are optimized to provide the appropriate means and opportunity. If one looks at the means and opportunities that are necessary to generate power, we find that in the case of familiar situations/tasks it is likely that assets will be in the right place (or arrangements will be have been made to move them into position). Information needs, as formally expressed by the essential elements of information and information exchange requirements, are likely to be well known. Thus, it is likely that the right information will be provided to the right entities at the right time. In the cognitive domain, familiar situations are well understood and so it is likely that responsible individuals will be able to make sense of the situation. Finally, organizational processes and rules of engagement have been developed and refined to meet the needs of familiar situations. Therefore, it is likely that individuals and entities will know how to work together to get the job done.

All of this changes when hierarchies are faced with unfamiliar tasks or the need to perform in an unfamiliar situation. While individuals may be agile enough to adapt, hierarchies are not as agile. This is because existing systems and processes have been designed to provide and process the information necessary and to involve the people and organizations that are required. Unfamiliar tasks, by their very nature, are those where interactions among stovepipes are important. In this case, provisions will not have been known and made in advance. Hence, the information needed may not be known, the information may not be available, if it is available the owner of the information may not know who needs it, and the systems may not be designed to get the information to those who need it. A similar situation exists with respect to the means to accomplish an unfamiliar task. Thus, the ability of a hierarchy to provide its human resources, the "instruments" of power (the means and opportunities listed in Figure 30, reproduced from Chapter 9 for the reader's convenience), while excellent in the case of familiar situations and tasks, is very limited in the case of unfamiliar situations and tasks.

Another property of organizations that affects power is agility, particularly the component of resiliency. Carley et al. have employed social network analysis and multiagent models[7] to explore how and to what extent organizations can

	Means	Opportunity
Physical	Organic Resources	The right actions The right places at the right times
Information	Organic Information	The right information at the right time
Cognitive	Knowledge and ability	The right understandings at the right time
Social	Access to information	The right rules of engagement and partners at the right time
	Command Authority	The right distribution of command intent at the right time

Figure 30. The Sources of Power as a Function of Domain

be destabilized by removing key leaders (or emergent leaders). They compared a "stylized hierarchical centralized network" with a "stylized distributed decentralized network" and found that it was more difficult to destabilize a distributed decentralized network.

A rigorous comparison of current vs. potential network-centric organizational forms really needs to wait until we have a chance to explore new command...control...approaches and organizations in analyses, models, simulations, experiments, and operations. However, based upon existing research, we can expect organizations that are based upon *power to the edge* principles and that conduct network-centric operations to be more agile.

NOTES

1   Opportunities can also be created by agile organizations. This in turn increases power.

2   With the exception of offensive Information Operations, which makes this capability also directly related to the ability of the organization to utilize information.

3   For example, precision guided bombs are arguably more cost effective (need to use less of them and the related savings in tail) and can be employed in situations where dumb bombs cannot be employed.

4   These constraints exist as a result of (1) the limitations that hierarchies place on information flows, (2) existing patterns of authority and responsibilities, and (3) restrictions on interactions.

5   Hogg, Tad, and Bernardo A. Huberman. "Communities of Practice: Performance and Evaluation." *Computational and Mathematical Organization Theory.* No 1. Norwell, MA: Kluwer Academic Publishers. 1995. pp. 73-92. Carley, Kathleen M. "A Theory of Group Stability." *American Sociological Review.* Vol 56, Iss 3. JSTOR, American Sociological Association. Jun 1991. pp. 331-354.

6   This is true for successful hierarchies, ones that have evolved under competitive pressures.

7   Carley, Kathleen M., Ju-Sung Lee, and David Krackhardt. "Destabilizing Networks." *Connections*. No 24(3): 79-92. British Colombia, CAN: INSNA. 2002.

Chapter 13

Edge-Oriented Mission Capability Packages

The concept of mission capability packages has now been around for almost a decade.[1] Inherent within MCPs is the recognition of the need to coevolve each of the components (doctrine, command, education, training, and systems) of such a package.[2] Secretary of Defense Donald Rumsfeld has stated that "a revolution in military affairs is about more than building new high-tech weapons, though that is certainly part of it. It's also about new ways of thinking, and new ways of fighting."[3] To be successful, this effort must address processes and strategies as much as systems and tools. A failure to appropriately coevolve MCP components will not only result in lost capabilities, but can also result in a degradation of performance. In this case, there will be a failure to take full advantage of new and improved means and increased opportunities (power foregone), as well as the possibility of an actual loss of power.

Therefore, the adoption of *power to the edge* as a command and control, organizational, architectural, and behavioral principle implies that other components of MCPs will be coevolved to reflect *power to the edge* principles. This chapter discusses the nature of the changes that need to take place to other key elements of MCPs and the institutional processes that conceive, develop, and support them.

COEVOLUTION OF INSTITUTIONAL PROCESSES

Currently fielded capabilities are usually a product of DoD's stovepiped planning, budgeting, and acquisition processes (all of which are material-dominated) and a requirements process that is backward looking. While power is currently distributed, being vested in the Services and Agencies, this power topology is clearly antithetical to jointness and far from the warfighter edge. Over the years, there have been numerous attempts to improve the system to make it more joint and responsive to warfighters' needs. To date, these efforts have been only marginally successful because they have not fundamentally transformed these processes into edge-oriented ones. The adoption of an edge-oriented approach to the main function of DoD, the conduct of military operations, demands that these supporting processes be transformed as well.

STRATEGIC PLANNING AND REQUIREMENTS

Planning for the future is as important in the Information Age as ever before, but the objective and nature of this activity is markedly different for edge organizations than it is for traditional hierarchies. In the Industrial Age, everyone had faith that even the most challenging of problems could be successfully tackled by a systematic approach. This approach consisted of decomposition, specialization, and then optimization of the components. This worked well enough when the interactions among the components did not dominate and when the rate of change in the conditions was in line with the responsiveness of the organization. Thus, even though hierarchies are relatively slow, they could keep pace with a fairly stable security environment, which was characteristic of most of the 20th century.

With the coming of the Information Age, security problems became more complex and situations much more dynamic. Prediction under these circumstances becomes problematic and so does the traditional approach to strategic planning. This traditional approach, threat-based planning, has until recently been firmly entrenched in DoD. Very recently,[4] DoD has shifted to a capability-based planning approach. While this is a step in the right direction, as currently practiced this approach still retains many of the undesirable characteristics of the former approach. The issue at hand is (1) what capabilities to pursue and (2) how these decisions will be made.

First, the good news: there has been a strategic decision to put in place the information-related capabilities that would enable a *power to the edge* approach. These capabilities include vastly improved connectivity for all force entities and the entities that support them, increased bandwidth, increased interoperability to break down information and process stovepipes, and collaborative environments. The move from first establishing a need (requirement) for an information exchange (IER) and then satisfying this requirement on a case-by-case basis to the acceptance of a need for universal connectivity and wide-spread interoperability represents a fundamental shift in the approach to strategic planning. It is a shift from the assumption that you can predict who needs to talk to or work with whom to the recognition that we need a robustly networked force[5] to be able to deal with situations as they arise.

This recognition and acceptance that prediction has become futile has, unfortunately, not carried over to the planning and requirements processes for other material and nonmaterial investments. There is still a widespread belief that the future is a linear extension of the past, that what worked before will continue to work. This has resulted in an emphasis on modernization and incremental innovation rather than on real transformation, despite proponents of transformation at the highest levels.

The continued emphasis on specifying requirements in advance and acquiring capability material on a project-by-project basis forces us to predict when predictions cannot be reliably made. This is analogous to an insistence on traditional command and control approaches (centralized planning and adaptive control processes) when these approaches cannot recognize changes in the situation quickly enough and/or cannot respond to them fast enough. Just as we advocate exploring and adopting an Information Age approach to command and control (as articulated in Chapter 11) that recognizes how control needs to be an emergent property, we are in favor of a new approach to strategic planning that seeks to establish the conditions necessary to create, nurture, and bring to fruition disruptive innovation.

A private sector development that mirrors this thinking came to our attention as this book was being written. In the 9th issue of *Perspectives on Business Innovation*,[6] Meyer and Davis[7] argue that connectivity in the environment has accelerated change and increased volatility. This results in more rapid and varied adaptation and fewer and shorter periods of stability conducive to achieving efficient solutions. The situation they describe is clearly less and less conducive to prediction and to preplanned responses. They argue for what they call the Adaptive Enterprise. Both *power to the edge* and the Adaptive Enterprise reject engineering in favor of the biological metaphor of evolution because of the need for continuing innovation. Both lead to the conclusion that Information Age organizations need to experiment rather than plan. Concept-based experimentation should drive the manner in which an organization responds to a challenge.

EXPERIMENTATION, COEVOLUTION, AND POWER TO THE EDGE

Experimentation should also drive requirements for the various components of MCPs as these packages are coevolved. In addition to a *power to the edge* approach to organization, command and control, information dissemination, and infostructure architecture, how DoD approaches experimentation itself needs to reflect a *power to the edge* philosophy. *The Code of Best Practice for Experimentation*[8] identifies the various kinds of experimentation activities that need to be orchestrated as part of a concept-based experimentation campaign to conceive, refine, and fully mature innovation. The process suggested in *Information Age Transformation*[9] for coevolving MCPs was designed to replace current requirements, acquisition, exercise and training, and test and evaluation processes. This process is an explicit acknowledgement of the need to move away from a centralized, top-down, engineering-oriented process to a process that works bottom-up; one that creates fertility, seeds ideas, nurtures them, selects the most promising, weeds out the losers, and fertilizes the winners.[10] Only an empirically-based experimentation process that employs an appropriate set of measures[11] can accomplish this.

BEYOND TRAINING AND EXERCISES TO EDUCATION AND EXPERIMENTATION

In an attempt to innovate within a zone of comfort and get improved capability to the field far more quickly, some DoD organizations have tried to marry experimentation with exercises. The redesign of traditional exercises into activities that can be incubators of innovation has proven to have value, but the use of exercises, even recast to permit more freedom of action, should be considered to complement rather than substitute for a more comprehensive approach to experimentation. This is because experimentation within an exercise context cannot provide sufficient degrees of freedom to produce truly disruptive innovation, nor can it adequately train individuals and organizations in *power to the edge* principles and practices.

The bulk of exercises and training have coevolved to their present state based upon a set of Industrial Age assumptions. They are largely scripted events to develop proficiency in selected tasks or with selected systems (it is assumed that the "best" ways to accomplish these tasks are already known). Even when conducted with a need for experimentation in mind, they have, to date, permitted only very limited changes in work processes and command and control approaches, and are able to explore only a limited set of circumstances. For example, there have been numerous attempts to introduce

Information Operations into exercises. The disruptions and uncertainties that information attacks create have frequently resulted in IO not being played. In addition, constraints are often placed on those playing adversary forces. Again, the rationale behind their prohibitions is that without these constraints on behavior, training will be disrupted.

In Millennium Challenge 02 (MC02),[12] an event that was referred to sometimes as an exercise and sometimes as an experiment, the adversary forces acted in an unexpected manner. As is often the case with exercises, the event was stopped and the force reset. The behavior of adversary forces was further constrained for the rest of the exercise. This is not to say that no value came out of MC02, but rather that one needs to understand the limits of exercises in informing and preparing for DoD's transformation to a *power to the edge* enterprise.

The inherent conflicts between exercises, training, and *power to the edge* experimentation are not clearly understood by many involved in these activities. The conflicts stem from differences in perspectives regarding goals. The goals and assumptions associated with a training event, as currently articulated, are quite different from those of experimentation. If you believe you know how best to do something, you clearly want to teach it and practice it. This is the basis for current approaches to training and exercises. However, if you reject this assumption and instead believe that even if we knew the "best" way to do something, that it would not be best for long (an acceptance of the rapidity of change, adversary adaptation, etc.), then training and exercises must, at the very least, be accompanied by education and experimentation. This implies that, in addition to teaching "the way we know," we also need to educate individuals and create organizations to experiment, learn, and adapt.[13]

Some fear that an emphasis on experimentation will delay the fielding of new capabilities. This need not and should not be the case. What they do not understand is that experimentation is an integral and ongoing part of a *power to the edge* enterprise. Experimentation (the creation of variety and competitive pressure) is the fundamental mechanism needed to cope with change and fuel adaptation. Exercises, to the extent that they do not create as much variety, do not adequately analyze results, do not reflect the principles of *power to the edge*, and do not contribute as much to progress as a vigorous program of experimentation. Exercises can be valuable as a source of innovation. However, because it occurs in the context of current organization, current doctrine, and specific scenarios of interest, innovation in exercises represents the incremental modernization path to the future, not the transformational path.

NOTES

1   Mission Capability Packages were first proposed in 1995.
    http://www.dodccrp.org/MissCap.htm. (Apr 1, 2003)
    Alberts, David S. *Mission Capability Packages*. Washington, DC: NDU Press Publications. January 1995.
    Alberts, *Information Age Transformation*. pp. 74-77.

2   Alberts, *Unintended Consequences*.

3   CNN. January 31, 2002.
    http://www.cnn.com/2002/US/01/31/rumsfeld.speech/?related. (Apr 1, 2003)

4   *The Quadrennial Defense Review 2001*. Office of the Secretary of Defense, 30 September 2001.
    http://www.comw.org/qdr/qdr2001.pdf. (Apr 1, 2003)
    Wolfowitz Addresses Changing Defense Priorities. Jim Garamone American Forces

Press Service.
http://www.defenselink.mil/news/Nov2001/
n11162001_200111163.html. (Apr 1, 2003)
Conetta, Carl. "The Pentagon's New Budget, New Strategy, and New War." *Project on Defense Alternatives Briefing Report*. No 12. June 25, 2002.
http://www.comw.org/pda/0206newwar.html#footnote9. (Apr 1, 2003)

5   A robustly networked force is the "if" of the first tenet of NCW.

6   Meyer, "Embracing Evolution."

7   Christopher Meyer & Stan Davis are co-authors of *Future Wealth* and *Blur*. The material this is drawn from was adapted from drafts of a forthcoming book on the convergence of Information Technology, Biology, and Business.
Meyer, Christopher, and Stan Davis. *Future Wealth*. Boston, MA: Harvard Business School Press. 2000.
Meyer, Christopher, and Stan Davis. *Blur: The Speed of Change in the Connected Economy*. New York, NY: Little Brown & Company. 1999.

8   CCRP, *Experimentation*. pp. 24-60.

9   Alberts, *Information Age Transformation*. p. 75.

10   Meyer & Davis express this idea a bit differently. They call for a set of diverse experiments, the application of selective pressure, and riding the winners.

11   *Network Centric Warfare Conceptual Framework*. Network Centric Warfare and Network Enabled Capabilities Workshop: Overview of Major Findings. Dec 17-19, 2002. OSD(NII) in conjunction with RAND and EBR, Inc.

12   Plummer, Anne. "Expeditionary Test." *Air Force Magazine*. Arlington, VA: Air Force Association. November 2002. p. 54.
Schrage, Michael. "Military Overkill Defeats Virtual War; And Real-World Soldiers Are the Losers." *The Washington Post*. Washington, DC: The Washington Post Company. September 22, 2002.

13   Senge, P. *The Fifth Discipline: The Art and Practice of the Learning Organization*. New York, NY: Doubleday. 1990.

Chapter 14

The Way Ahead

As understanding of the true scope and nature of an Information Age transformation spreads through DoD and the Defense community both here and abroad, the need to adopt the principles of *power to the edge* will become increasingly clear. As a result, there will be ever increasing support for the enablers of transformation. These include increased connectivity and interoperability, more collaborative processes, and real experimentation.

The introduction of change into any population is a phased phenomenon. The first step involves the creation of the new idea or capability. The second is the recognition of the value of the idea/capability by a group of individuals called *early adopters*. Next, influential *opinion leaders* get behind the idea. This is followed by more adoption. As adoption spreads, the barriers fall and the cost and risks of adoption decrease. A positive feedback loop is created and finally all except the *recalcitrants* adopt. To speed things along, in the case of *power to the edge*, the information-related capabilities (the infostructure) need to be put in place. Then when the desire to share, collaborate, and explore *power to the edge* principles reaches a critical mass, nothing will prevent such activity.[1]

Getting to this point will take time. It has been more than 4 years since the tenets of NCW began to be widely discussed, yet there remains a fair amount of misunderstanding and misinformation circulating about what NCW is and is not. The ambiguity of the English language, the very different sets of experiences and expertise that abound in DoD, and the lack of a single accepted, authoritative voice contribute to the confusion. Cognitive dissonance, a natural human response to information or ideas that do not square with existing knowledge or beliefs, often results in individuals misconstruing or misunderstanding concepts and policies. Therefore, an important step on DoD's road to becoming an *edge organization* involves efforts to improve the level of understanding that exists within DoD of the *power to the edge* principles involved. This book is meant to contribute to this desired end.

Given the significant advances in technology, the primary barriers that remain are cultural and institutional. Finding ways to remove these impediments to progress is on the critical path to transformation. Education alone will not be sufficient. The reward and value structures need to change in order to establish new cultural and institutional norms that (at the very least) permit exploration of *power to the edge* principles (for example, desirable attitudes and behaviors about sharing information, collaboration, loyalty, and relationships within an organization and among organizations). There must be proper incentives associated with these desirable behaviors.

Measurement plays an important role in accelerating understanding. The continued development and refinement of a Network Centric Warfare Conceptual Framework[2] (with measures in the physical, information, cognitive, and social domains) is a critical activity, as is the widespread employment of this conceptual framework.

In addition, significantly more attention and resources need to focus on research and experimentation. The diversity of organizational and institutional perspectives within DoD provides a robust structure for creating, critiquing, improving, and implementing *power to the edge* and Network Centric Warfare. However, without a rigorous program of research and experimentation, any effort to develop and apply new knowledge will fail. An agenda that enables different organizations and institutions to focus their efforts in their areas of expertise encourages edge interactions and demands jointness not only at the top but throughout,[3] and will help to speed the process. This agenda should include all the key elements of the NCW Conceptual Framework:

- Exploring the meaning of a "robustly networked force;"

- Examining the mechanisms by which information sharing and collaboration improve the quality of information;

- Understanding how sensemaking (shared awareness, shared understandings, and authoritative shared decisionmaking) works in *power to the edge* organizations;

- Exploring the educational, training, and doctrinal implications of adopting *power to the edge* organizational principles;

- Developing modeling and simulation tools that can represent the full range of the spectrum of C2 approaches;

- Understanding the necessary conditions for and consequences of adopting self-synchronization; and

- Documenting through case studies the experience of those forces and force elements applying network-centric and *power to the edge* principles in recent conflicts, peacekeeping, and nation building missions.

DoD's transformation is not in doubt. The remaining questions involve how long will it take and the specific details of DoD's adaptation to the Information Age. Looking back from 2050, it will seem planned and orderly. From our vantage point in 2003, it appears more chaotic. Ultimately, much of the leadership in this direction will come from the edge—the warfighters and pioneers in how to create and exploit information advantages.

NOTES

1   Mandeles, Mark. "Military Revolutions During Peacetime: Organizational Innovation and Emerging Weapons Technologies." Office of Net Assessment. 1995.
http://members.aol.com/novapublic/prod02.htm. (Apr 1, 2003)

2   Network Centric Warfare Conceptual Framework. Network Centric Warfare and Network Enabled Capabilities Workshop: Overview of Major Findings. Dec 17-19, 2002. OSD(NII) in conjunction with RAND and EBR, Inc.

3   From President to Private.

Bibliography

ABCA. *Coalition Operations Handbook*. American-British-Canadian-Australian Program. 2001. http://www.abca.hqda.pentagon.mil/Publications/COH/ABCA-COH.PDF. (May 1, 2003)

Ackerman, Robert K. "Special Forces Become Network-Centric." *SIGNAL Magazine*. Fairfax, VA: AFCEA. March 2003. http://us.net/signal/Archive/March03/special-march.html. (May 1, 2003)

Alberts, David S. *Information Age Transformation: Getting to a 21st Century Military*. Washington, DC: CCRP Publication Series. 2002.

Alberts, David S. *Mission Capability Packages*. Washington, DC: National Defense University. 1995.

Alberts, David S., John J. Garstka, Richard E. Hayes, and David T. Signori. *Understanding Information Age Warfare*. Washington, DC: CCRP Publication Series. 2001.

Alberts, David S., and Daniel S. Papp. *Information Age Anthology, Volume I: The Nature of the Information Age*. Washington, DC: CCRP Publication Series. 2001.

Alberts, David S., and Richard E. Hayes. *Command Arrangements for Peace Operations*. Washington, DC: NDU Press Publication. 1995.

Alberts, David S., John J. Garstka, Richard E. Hayes, and David T. Signori. *The Unintended Consequences of Information Age Technologies*. Washington, DC: CCRP Publication Series. 1996.

Alberts, David S., John J. Garstka, and Frederick P. Stein. *Network Centric Warfare: Developing and Leveraging Information Superiority*. Washington, DC: CCRP Publication Series. 1999.

Allard, Kenneth. *Somalia Operations: Lessons Learned*. Washington, DC: CCRP Publication Series. 1995.

ASD(NII) CIO Homepage. Department of Defense. http://www.c3i.osd.mil/homepage.html#goals. (Apr 1, 2003)

Bacon, Sir Francis. *Meditationes Sacrae*. 1597.

Bakel, Rogier van. "Origin's Original." *Wired*. Issue 4.11. New York, NY: Wired News. 1996.

Bell, Chip R. "Picking Super Service Personnel." *Supervisory Management*. Vol 35, Iss 6. Saranac Lake. Jun 1990.

Bigley, G.A., and Roberts, K.H. "The Incident Command System: High Reliability Organizing for Complex and Volatile Task Environments." *Academy of Management Journal*. Vol 44, No 6. 2001.

Blanchard, Eugene. *Introduction to Networking and Data Communications*. Calgary, AL: Southern Alberta Institute of Technology. 2000.

Bohnenberger, Thorsten. "Recommendation Planning Under Uncertainty: Consequences of Inaccurate Probabilities." Saarbrucken, GER: Department of Computer Science, Saarland University. 2001. http://orgwis.gmd.de/~gross/um2001ws/papers/position_papers/bohnenberger.pdf. (Apr 1, 2003)

Bonabeau, Eric. "When Intuition is Not Enough." *Perspectives on Business Innovation*. Issue 9. Cambridge, MA: Center for Business Innovation. Spring 2003. http://www.cbi.cgey.com/journal/issue9/when_intuition.htm. (Mar 31, 2003)

Borck, James. "Building Your Site from Scratch." *InfoWorld*. Framingham. Oct 4, 1999.

Bowden, Mark. *Black Hawk Down: A Story of Modern War*. New York, NY: Penguin. 2000.

Bragg, Terry. "Ten Ways to Deal with Conflict." *IIE Solutions*. Norcross. Oct 1999.

Bush, President George W. "Statement by the President in his Address to the Nation." Office of the Press Secretary. September 11, 2001. http://www.whitehouse.gov/news/releases/2001/09/20010911-16.html. (May 1, 2003)

Bush, President George W. "The National Security Strategy of the United States of America." White House. September 2002. http://www.whitehouse.gov/nsc/nss.pdf. (May 1, 2003)

Bushardt, Stephen C., David L. Duhon, and Aubrey R. Fowler, Jr. "Management Delegation Myths and the Paradox of Task Assignment." *Business Horizons.* Greenwich. Mar/Apr 1991.

Cabral, Ana Maria Rezende. "Participatory Management." Anthony Vaughn. *International Reader in the Management of Library, Information and Archive Services.* Paris, FR: UNESCO. 1986.

Capstone Requirements Document (CRD). *Global Information Grid (GIG).* March 28, 2001. http://www.dfas.mil/ technology/pal/regs/gigcrdflaglevelreview.pdf. (Apr 1, 2003)

Carley, Kathleen M. "A Theory of Group Stability." *American Sociological Review.* Vol 56, Iss 3. JSTOR, American Sociological Association. Jun 1991.

Carley, Kathleen M., Ju-Sung Lee, and David Krackhardt. "Destabilizing Networks." *Connections.* No 24(3): 79-92. British Colombia, CAN: INSNA. 2002.

Cebrowski, VADM Arthur K., and John J. Garstka. "Network-Centric Warfare: Its Origin and Future" *Proceedings.* Volume 124/1/1,139. Annapolis, MD: U.S. Naval Institute. 1998.

Chief Information Officer (DOD-CIO). *Net-Centric Data Strategy.* Washington, DC: Department of Defense. May 9, 2003.

"CIMIC Reconstruction." *NATO Review.* Vol 49, No 1. Brussels; NATO. Spring 2001. http://www.nato.int/docu/review/2001/0101-06.htm. (Apr 1, 2003)

Clark, W.K. *Waging Modern War.* New York, NY: Perseus Books. 2001.

Clausewitz, Carl von. Michael E. Howard and Peter Paret, eds. *On War.* Princeton, NJ: Princeton University Press. 1976.

Command and Control Research Program. *The Code of Best Practice for Experimentation.* Washington, DC: CCRP Publication Series. 2002.

Coram, Robert. *Boyd: The Fighter Pilot Who Changed the Art of War.* Boston: Little Brown & Company. 2002.

Coutu, Diane L. "How Resilience Works." *Harvard Business Review.* Boston, MA: Harvard Business School Press. May 2002.

Creveld, Martin van. *Command in War.* Cambridge, MA: Harvard University Press. 1985.

Creveld, Martin van. *The Transformation of War.* New York, NY: The Free Press. 1991.

Czerwinski, Tom. *Coping with the Bounds: Speculations on Non-Linearity in Military Affairs.* Washington, DC: CCRP Publication Series. 1998.

Davenport, T.H. and Prusack, L. *Working Knowledge: How Organizations Manage What They Know.* Cambridge, MA: Harvard Business School Press. 1998.

Davidson, Lisa Witzig, Margaret Daly Hayes, and James J. Landon. Humanitarian and Peace Operations: NGOs and the Military in the Interagency Process. Washington, DC: CCRP Publication Series. 1996.

Davis, Paul K. "Institutionalizing Planning for Adaptiveness." in Paul K. Davis, ed., *New Challenges for Defense Planning— Rethinking How Much Is Enough.* Santa Monica, CA: RAND, MR-400-RC. 1994c.

Defense Systems, Inc. *Headquarters Effectiveness Program Summary Task 002.* Arlington, VA: C3 Architecture and Mission Analysis, Planning and Systems Integration Directorate, Defense Communications Agency. 1983.

Department of Defense. http://www.c3i.osd.mil/org/cio/doc/GPM11-8450.pdf. (March 27, 2003)

Department of Defense Dictionary of Military and Associated Terms. Joint Pubs. 1-02. http://www.dtic.mil/doctrine/jel/doddict/. (Apr 1, 2003)

Dixon, Norman F. *On the Psychology of Military Incompetence.* New York, NY: Basic Books. 1976.

Elmquist, Michael. "CIMIC in East Timor: An account of civil-military cooperation, coordination and collaboration in the early phases of the East Timor relief operation." UN Office for the Coordination of Humanitarian Affairs (OCHA). 1999. http://wwwnotes.reliefweb.int/files/rwdomino.nsf/ 4c6be8192aef259cc12564f500422b3c/ 313ad8c125d1212cc125684f004a48bd?OpenDocument (Apr 1, 2003)

Ferguson, Homer, and Owen Brewster. "Minority Pearl Harbor Report." Joint Committee on the Investigation of the Pearl Harbor Attack, Congress of the United States. Pursuant to S. Con. Res. 27. *Investigation of the Pearl Harbor*

Attack. 79th Congress, 2nd Session. Washington, DC: Government Printing Office. 1946. http://www.ibiblio.org/pha/pha/congress/part_0.html. (May 1, 2003)

Fontana, John. "Denial-of-service attacks cripple Microsoft for second day." *Network WorldFusion*. January 25, 2001.

Friedman, Thomas. *The Lexus and the Olive Tree*. New York, NY: Anchor Books. 2000.

Gallis, Paul E. "Kosovo: Lessons Learned from Operation *Allied Force*." Congressional Research Service Report to Congress, The Library of Congress. November 19, 1999. http://www.au.af.mil/au/awc/awcgate/crs/rl30374.pdf. (May 1, 2003)

Garamone, Jim. "Army Tests Land Warrior for 21st Century Soldier." *American Forces Press Service*. Department of Defense DefenseLink. http://www.defenselink.mil/news/Sep1998/9809117b.jpg. (Apr 1, 2003)

Garstka, John J. "Network Centric Warfare: An Overview of Emerging Theory." *PHALANX*. Alexandria, VA: MORS. 2000.

Giambastiani, ADM Edmund P. Jr. *Statement of the Commander United States Joint Forces Command Before The House Armed Services Committee*, United States House of Representatives. March 12, 2003. http://www.jfcom.mil/newslink/storyarchive/2003/pa031203.htm. (Apr 1, 2003)

Glantz, David M. *The Role of Soviet Intelligence in Soviet Military Strategy in WWII*. Novato, CA: Presidio Press. 1990.

Goldwater Nichols Department of Defense Reorganization Act of 1986.
National Defense University.
http://www.ndu.edu/library/goldnich/goldnich.html.
(Mar 21, 2003)

Gove, Philip Babcock, ed. *Webster's Third New International Dictionary.* Springfield, MA: Merriam-Webster, Inc. 2002.

Graham, Bradley, and Vernon Loeb. "An Air War of Might, Coordination and Risks." *The Washington Post.* Apr 27, 2003.

Gray, Robert. "Cultivating the Customer: Reaping the Rewards of the Supply Chain." *Perspectives on Business Innovation.* Issue 9. Cambridge, MA: Center for Business Innovation. Spring 2003. http://www.cbi.cgey.com/journal/issue9/not_all.htm. (Mar 31, 2003)

Greenberg, Jeanne and Herbert M., Ph.D. "The Personality Of A Top Salesperson." *Nation's Business.* December, 1983.

Grudin, Jonathan. *Group Dynamics and Ubiquitous Computing Association for Computing Machinery.* New York, NY: Communications of the ACM. Dec 2002.

Hamilton, Sir Ian, British Army. *The Soul and Body of an Army.* London: Arnold. 1922.

Hammonds, Keith H. "The Strategy of the Fighter Pilot." *Fast Company.* June 2002. p98. http://www.fastcompany.com/online/59/pilot.html. (May 1, 2003)

Harrison, David A, Kenneth H. Price, Joanne H. Gavin, Anna T. Florey. *Time, Teams, and Task Performance: Changing Effects of Surface - and Deep-level Diversity on Group Functioning.* Briarcliff Manor: Academy of Management Journal. Vol 45. Oct 2002.

Hayes, Richard E. "Systematic Assessment of C2 Effectiveness and its Determinates." Vienna, VA: Evidence Based Research, Inc. http://www.dodccrp.org/sm_workshop/pdf/ SAC2EID.pdf. (Apr 1, 2003)

Hayes, Richard, and Sue Iwanski. "Analyzing Effects Based Operations (EBO) Workshop Summary." *PHALANX*. Alexandria, VA: MORS. Vol 35, No 1. March 2002.

Hayes, Richard E., Mark Hainline, Conrad Strack, and Daniel Bucioni. *Theater Headquarters Effectiveness: Its Measurement and Relationship to Size Structure, Functions, and Linkage*. McLean, VA: Defense Systems, Inc. 1983.

Herman, Mark. *Measuring the Effects of Network-Centric Warfare*. Vol. 1. Director of Net Assessment, Office of the Secretary of Defense. McLean, VA: Booz Allen & Hamilton. April 28, 1999.

Herz, J.C. *Joystick Nation: How Videogames Ate Our Quarters, Won Our Hearts, and Rewired Our Minds*. New York, NY: Little, Brown & Company. 1997.

Hillier, Major General. Rick J. "Leadership Thoughts from Canada's Army: Follow Me." Keynote Address of the 7th International Command and Control Research and Technology Symposium. Quebec City, QC: Canada. September 16-20, 2002.

Hogg, Tad, and Bernardo A. Huberman. "Communities of Practice: Performance and Evaluation." *Computational and Mathematical Organization Theory*. No 1. Norwell, MA: Kluwer Academic Publishers. 1995.

Hughes, Wayne P. *Fleet Tactics - Theory and Practice*. Annapolis, MD: Naval Institute Press. 1986.

Hundley, Richard O. *Past Revolutions, Future Transformations: What Can the History of Revolutions in Military Affairs Tell Us About Transforming the U.S. Military?* Santa Monica, CA: RAND. 1999.

James, John, Brian Sayrs, V. S. Subrahmanian, and John Benton. "Uncertainty Management: Keeping Battlespace Visualization Honest." Lockheed Martin Advanced Technologies Laboratories & University of Maryland. 1999. http://www.atl.external.lmco.com/overview/papers/951-9864a.pdf. (Apr 1, 2003)

Janis, Irving. *Groupthink: Psychological Studies of Policy Decisions and Fiascoes*. Boston, MA: Houghton Mifflin College. 1982.

Jaques, Elliot. *Social Power and the CEO: Leadership and Trust in a Sustainable Free Enterprise System*. Westport, CT: Greenwood Publishing Group. 2002.

Jaques, Elliot. *A General Theory of Bureaucracy*. Hoboken, NJ: John Wiley & Sons. 1976.

Joint Expeditionary Forces Exercise, U.S. Air Force. http://afeo.langley.af.mil/gateway/jefx00.asp. (Feb 1, 2003)

Joint Military Operations Historical Collection. Washington, DC: Joint Chiefs of Staff. July 15, 1997. http://www.dtic.mil/doctrine/jel/history/hist.pdf. (Apr 1, 2003)

Joint Vision 2010. Chairman of the Joint Chiefs of Staff. Washington, DC: Joint Chiefs of Staff. 1996.

Jomini, General Baron Antione Henri. "The Command of Armies and the Supreme Control of Operations." *Precis de l'Art de Guerre.* Chapter 2. Article 14. 1838.
Jomini, Antione Henri. *The Art of War.* New York, NY: Greenhill Press. 1996.

Kalat, J. W. *Biological Psychology.* Pacific Grove, CA: Brooks/Cole. 1998.

Katzenbach, Jon R. and Douglas K. Smith. *The Discipline of Teams: A Mindbook-Workbook for Delivering Small Group Performance.* New York, NY: John Wiley & Sons, Inc. 2001.

Keegan, John. *The Mask of Command.* New York, NY: Viking Penguin. 1988.

Klein, Gary. *Why Developing Your Gut Instincts Will Make You Better at What You Do.* New York, NY: Doubleday and Company, Inc. 2002.

Klein, Gary, and Eduardo Salas. *Linking Expertise and Naturalistic Decision Making.* Mahwah, NJ: Lawrence Erlbaum Assoc. 2001.

Klein, Gary. *Sources of Power: How People Make Decisions.* Cambridge, MA: MIT Press. 1998.

Krulak, Charles. "The Strategic Corporal: Leadership in the Three Block War." *Marine Corps Gazette.* Vol 83, No 1. January 1999.

Kwak, Chris, and Robert Fagin. *Internet 3.0. Equity Research Technology.* New York, NY: Bear Stearns. 2001. https://access.bearstearns.com/supplychain/infrastructure.pdf. (Feb 1, 2003)

Leavitt, Harold J., and Homa Bahrami. *Managerial Psychology: Managing Behavior in Organizations*. Chicago, IL: University of Chicago Press. 1988.

Leavitt, Harold J. "Some Effect of Certain Communication Patterns on Group Performance." *Journal of Abnormal and Social Psychology*. Washington, DC: American Psychological Society. 1951.

Lee, Elan. "This is Not a Game: A Discussion of the Creation of the AI Web Experience." Presented at the 16th annual Game Developers Conference. March 19-23, 2002.

Leedom, Dennis K. "Sensemaking Experts Panel Meeting Final Report." Vienna, VA: EBR, Inc. June 2002.

Leedom, Dennis K. "Sensemaking Symposium Final Report." Vienna, VA: EBR, Inc. October 2001.

Leopold, George. "Networks: DoD's First Line of Defense." *Tech Web*. Seattle, WA: CMP Media. October 1997.

Lewandowski, CAPT Linda. "Sense and Respond Logistics: The Fundamentals of Demand Networks." U.S. Navy Office of the Secretary of Defense, Office of Force Transformation. Jeffrey R. Cares Alidade Incorporated. 2002.

Madrick, Jeff. "The Business Media and the New Economy." Research Paper R-24. Boston, MA: Harvard University Press. 2001. p7. http://www.ksg.harvard.edu/presspol/publications/R-24Madrick.PDF. (Apr 1, 2003)

Mandeles, Mark. "Military Revolutions During Peacetime: Organizational Innovation and Emerging Weapons Technologies." Office of Net Assessment. 1995. http://members.aol.com/novapublic/prod02.htm. (Apr 1, 2003)

Mankin, Eric, and Prabal Chakrabarti. "Valuing Adaptability: Markers for Managing Financial Volatility." *Perspectives on Business Innovation*. Issue 9. Cambridge, MA: Center for Business Innovation. Spring 2003. http://www.cbi.cgey.com/journal/issue9/not_all.htm. (Mar 31, 2003)

McCollum, Sean. "America on Wheels." *Scholastic Update*. New York, NY. Feb 7, 1997.

Merriam Webster's Collegiate® Dictionary, 10th Edition. Springfield, MA: Merriam-Webster, Inc. 1998.

Meyer, Christopher, and Stan Davis. *Future Wealth*. Boston, MA: Harvard Business School Press. 2000.

Meyer, Christopher, and Stan Davis. *Blur: The Speed of Change in the Connected Economy*. New York, NY: Little Brown & Company. 1999.

Meyer, Christopher, and Stan Davis. "Embracing Evolution: Business from the Bottom Up." *Perspectives on Business Innovation*. Issue 9. Cambridge, MA: Center for Business Innovation. Spring 2003.

Millennium Challenge 02. U.S. Joint Forces Command. http://www.jfcom.mil/about/experiments/mc02.htm. (Feb 1, 2003)

Miller, G.A. "The magical number seven, plus or minus two: Some limits on our capacity for processing information." *The Psychological Review.* Vol 63. 1956.

Mintzberg, Henry. *Mintzberg on Management: Inside Our Strange World of Organizations.* New York, NY: The Free Press. 1988.

Moffat, James. *Complexity Theory and Network Centric Warfare.* Washington, DC: CCRP Publication Series. 2003. Ministry of Defence. "Kosovo: Lessons from the Crisis." Presented to Parliament by the Secretary of State for Defence by Command of Her Majesty. June 2000. http://www.mod.uk/publications/kosovo_lessons/contents.htm. (May 1, 2003)

Money, Arthur L. *Report on Network Centric Warfare.* http://www.c3i.osd.mil/NCW/ncw_sense.pdf. (Feb 1, 2003)

NATO SAS026. *NATO Code of Best Practice for C2 Assessment.* Washington, DC: CCRP Publication Series. 2003.

Neck, Christopher P; Manz, Charles C. *From Groupthink to Teamthink: Toward the Creation of Constructive Thought Patterns in Self-managing Work Teams.* New York, NY: Human Relations. 1994.

Network Centric Warfare Department of Defense Report to Congress. July 2001. http://www.dodccrp.org/NCW/NCW_report/report/ncw_cover.html. (Apr 1, 2003)

Olmstead, J.A., M.J. Baranick and B.L. Elder. *Research on Training for Brigade Command Groups: Factors Contributing to Unit Combat Readiness (Technical Report TR-78-A18).* Alexandria, VA: U.S. Army Research Institute. 1978.

Peterson, Rolf O., Amy K. Jacobs, Thomas D. Drummer, L. David Mech, and Douglas W. Smith. "Leadership behavior in relation to dominance and reproductive status in gray wolves, Canis lupus." *Canadian Journal of Zoology.* Ottawa, CAN: NRC Research Press. Aug 2002. http://canis.tamu.edu/wfscCourses/Examples/RefWolf.html. (May 1, 2003)

Petre, Peter. *General Norman Schwarzkopf: It Doesn't Take a Hero.* New York, NY: Bantom Books. 1992.

Petress, Ken. *Power: Definition, Typology, Description, Examples, and Implications.* http://www.umpi.maine.edu/~petress/power.pdf. (Feb 1, 2003)

Pierce, L.G. and E.K. Bowman. "Cultural barriers to teamwork in a multinational coalition environment." *23rd Army Science Conference.* Orlando, FL. Dec 2-5, 2002.

Pigeau, Ross, and Carol McCann. "Re-conceptualizing Command and Control." Kingston, ON: *Canadian Military Journal.* Vol 3, No 1. Spring 2002.

Plummer, Anne. "Expeditionary Test." *Air Force Magazine.* Arlington, VA: Air Force Association. November 2002.

Press Release by U.S. Senator Chuck Schumer. *Poor Communication Between FBI and Local Law Enforcement Threatens Public Safety.* Dec 11, 2001. http://schumer.senate.gov/1-Senator%20Schumer%20Website%20Files/pressroom/press_releases/PR00758.htm. (Apr 1, 2003)

Report of the DoD Commission on Beirut International Airport Terrorist Act, October 23, 1983. The Long Commission Report. 1983. http://www.ibiblio.org/hyperwar/AMH/XX/MidEast/ Lebanon-1982-1984/DOD-Report/index.html#toc. (Apr 1, 2003)

Rettinger, David A., and Reid Hastie. "Content effects on decision making." *Organizational Behavior and Human Decision Processes.* New York. Jul 2001.

Rice, Condoleezza. "The Party, the Military, and Decision Authority in the Soviet Union." *World Politics.* Baltimore, MD: Johns Hopkins Press. Vol 40, No 1. 1987.

Rinaldo, Richard. "Peace Operations: Perceptions." *A Common Perspective.* Joint Warfighting Center. Vol 7, No 2. 1999.

Roberts, Nancy. "Coping with the Wicked Problems: The Case of Afghanistan." Jones, L., J. Guthrie, and P. Steane, eds. *International Public Management Reform: Lessons from Experience.* London, ENG: Elsevier. 2001.

Robertson, Bruce, and Valentin Sribar. *The Adaptive Enterprise: IT Infrastructure Strategies to Manage Change and Enable Growth.* Santa Clara, CA: Intel Press. 2001.

Rogers, Amy. "Maximum Security." *Computer Reseller News.* Manhasset. Sep 20, 1999.

Rollender, Matt. "SSL: The secret handshake of the 'Net." *Network World.* Framingham. Feb 3, 2003.

Rumsfeld, Donald H. *Transformational Planning Guidance.* Department of Defense. April 2003.

Schrage, Michael. "Military Overkill Defeats Virtual War; And Real-World Soldiers Are the Losers." *The Washington Post*. Washington, DC: The Washington Post Company. September 22, 2002.

Siegel, Pascale Combelles. *Target Bosnia: Integrating Information Activities in Peace Operations. NATO-Led Operations in Bosnia-Herzegovina*. Washington, DC: CCRP Publication Series. 1998.

Simpson, D. Richard. "Doctrine -Who Needs It? You Do!" *Mobility Forum*. Scott AFB. May/Jun 1998.

Sinclair, Andrea L. *The Effects of Justice and Cooperation on Team Effectiveness*. Thousand Oaks: Small Group Research. Feb 2003.

Smith, Edward A. *Effects Based Operations: Applying Network Centric Warfare in Peace, Crisis, and War*. Washington, DC: CCRP Publication Series. 2003.

Smith, Preston G. "Managing Risk Proactively in Product Development Projects." Portland, OR: New Product Dynamics. 2002. http://www.newproductdynamics.com/ Risk/IPL921.pdf. (Apr 1, 2003)

Somalia Inquiry Report. Department of National Defence, CA. 1997. http://www.dnd.ca/somalia/somaliae.htm. (Feb 1, 2003)

Stein, Fred. "Observations on the Emergence of Network Centric Warfare." *Proceedings for the 1998 Command and Control Research and Technology Symposium*. Washington DC: CCRP Publication Series. 1998.

Stewart, Thomas A. "Right from the Gut: Investing with Naturalistic Decision Making." *The Consilient Observer.* Vol 1, Issue 22. Dec 3, 2002.

Sun Tzu. Thomas Cleary trans. *The Art of War.* Boston, MA: Shambhala Publications, Inc. 1991.

"The Bosnia-Herzegovina After Action Review I (BHAAR I) Conference Report." Carlisle Barracks, PA: United States Army Peacekeeping Institute (PKI). May 20-23, 1996. http://www.au.af.mil/au/awc/awcgate/lessons/ bhaar1.htm. (May 1, 2003)

Theater Headquarters Effectiveness: Its Measurement and Relationship to Size, Functions, and Linkages: Vol I: Measures of Effectiveness and Headquarters Effectiveness Assessment Tool. McLean, VA: Defense Systems, Inc.

Toffler, Alvin. *The Third Wave.* New York, NY: Bantam Books. 1991.

Toffler, Alvin. *War and Anti-War.* Boston, MA: Warner Books. 1995.

Trees, Harry L. L van. Detection, Estimation, and Modulation Theory, Optimum Array Processing. Hoboken, NJ: Wiley, John & Sons, Incorporated. March 2002.

Unified Vision 01. U.S. Joint Forces Command. http:// www.jfcom.mil/about/experiments/uv01.htm. (Feb 1, 2003)

United States Military Academy. History of the Academy. http://www.usma.edu/bicentennial/history/. (Feb 22, 2003)

United States Naval Academy. History of the Academy. http://www.usna.edu/VirtualTour/150years/. (Feb 22, 2003)

Urwick, L.F. "The Manager's Span of Control." *Harvard Business Review.* Cambridge, MA: Harvard Business Press. May-June 1958.

U.S. Conference of Mayors. *Status Report on Federal-Local Homeland Security Partnership.* September 2, 2002. http://www.usmayors.org/USCM/news/press_releases/documents/911_090902.asp. (Apr 1, 2003)

U.S. Army Research Institute for the Behavioral and Social Sciences. *The Army Command and Control Evaluation System Documentation.* Fort Leavenworth, KS: Research Unit. 1995.

Valentine Armouries. "Napoleonic uniform, 1807-1812 French Fusilier dress." Used with permission. http://www.varmouries.com/cloth/ccloth08.html. (Apr 1, 2003)

Verkerk, Maarten J., Jan De Leede, and Andre H.J. Nijhof. "From Responsible Management to Responsible Organizations: The Democratic Principle for Managing Organizational Ethics." *Business and Society Review.* New York, NY. Winter 2001.

Wall, Toby D., Paul R. Jackson, Sean Mullarkey, and Sharon K Parker. "The demands-control model of job strain: A more specific test." Leicester, UK: Journal of Occupational and Organizational Psychology. June 1996.

Weick, Karl E. "The Collapse of Sensemaking in Organizations: The Mann Gulch Disaster." *Administrative Science Quarterly.* Ithaca. Dec 1993.

Weick, K.E. & Sutcliffe, K.M. *Managing the Unexpected: Assuring High Performance in an Age of Complexity.* San Francisco, CA: Jossey-Wiley. 2001.

Wentz, Larry, ed. *Lessons from Bosnia: The IFOR Experience.* Washington, DC: CCRP Publication Series. 1998.

Wentz, Larry, ed. *Lessons from Kosovo: The KFOR Experience.* Washington, DC: CCRP Publication Series. 2002.

"Who is to Blame for the Bombing?" *New York Times.* Aug. 11, 1985.

Wilson, James Q. *Bureaucracy: What Government Agencies Do and Why They Do It.* New York, NY: Basic Books. 1991.

Woll, Johanna. "Not All Adaptive Enterprises are Alike." *Perspectives on Business Innovation.* Issue 9. Cambridge, MA: Center for Business Innovation. Spring 2003. http://www.cbi.cgey.com/journal/issue9/not_all.htm. (Mar 31, 2003)

Wykoff, Maj Michael D. "Shrinking the JTF Staff: Can We Reduce the Footprint Ashore?" Fort Leavenworth, KS: School of Advanced Military Studies, Command and General Staff College. Washington, DC: Storming Media. 1996.

Yam, Yaneer Bar. *Dynamics of Complex Systems.* New England Complex Systems Institute. Reading, MA: Addison-Wesley Publishing. 1997. http://necsi.org/publications/dcs/index.html (May 1, 2003)

About the Authors

Dr. David S. Alberts

Dr. Alberts is currently the Director, Research and Strategic Planning, OASD (NII). Prior to this he was the Director, Advanced Concepts, Technologies, and Information Strategies (ACTIS), Deputy Director of the Institute for National Strategic Studies, and the executive agent for DoD's Command and Control Research Program. This included responsibility for the Center for Advanced Concepts and Technology (ACT) and the School of Information Warfare and Strategy (SIWS) at the National Defense University. He has more than 25 years of experience developing and introducing leading-edge technology into private and public sector organizations. This extensive applied experience is augmented by a distinguished academic career in computer science, operations research, and Government service in senior policy and management positions. Dr. Alberts' experience includes serving as a CEO for a high-technology firm specializing in the design and development of large, state-of-the-art computer systems (including expert, investigative, intelligence, information, and command and control systems) in both Government and industry. He has also led organizations engaged in research and analysis of command and control system performance and related contributions to operational missions. Dr. Alberts has had policy responsibility for corporate computer and telecommunications capabilities, facilities, and experimental laboratories. His responsibilities have also included management of research aimed at enhancing the usefulness of systems, extending their productive life, and the development of improved methods for evaluating the contributions that systems make to organizational functions. Dr. Alberts frequently contributes to Government task forces and workshops on systems acquisition, command and control, and systems evaluation.

DR. RICHARD E. HAYES

As President and founder of Evidence Based Research, Inc., Dr. Hayes specializes in multidisciplinary analyses of command and control, intelligence, and national security issues; the identification of opportunities to improve support to decisionmakers in the defense and intelligence communities; the design and development of systems to provide that support; and the criticism, test, and evaluation of systems and procedures that provide such support. His areas of expertise include crisis management; political-military issues; research methods; experimental design; simulation and modeling; test and evaluation; military command, control, communication, and intelligence (NII); and decision-aiding systems. Since coming to Washington in 1974, Dr. Hayes has established himself as a leader in bringing the systematic use of evidence and the knowledge base of the social sciences into play in support of decisionmakers in the national security community, domestic agencies, and major corporations. He has initiated several programs of research and lines of business that achieved national attention and many others that directly influenced policy development in client organizations.

Dr. Richard E. Hayes

Catalog of CCRP Publications

Coalition Command and Control*
(Maurer, 1994)

Peace operations differ in significant ways from traditional combat missions. As a result of these unique characteristics, command arrangements become far more complex. The stress on command and control arrangements and systems is further exacerbated by the mission's increased political sensitivity.

The Mesh and the Net
(Libicki, 1994)

Considers the continuous revolution in information technology as it can be applied to warfare in terms of capturing more information (mesh) and how people and their machines can be connected (net).

Command Arrangements for Peace Operations
(Alberts & Hayes, 1995)

By almost any measure, the U.S. experience shows that traditional C2 concepts, approaches, and doctrine are not particularly well suited for peace operations. This book (1) explores the reasons for this, (2) examines alternative command arrangement approaches, and (3) describes the attributes of effective command arrangements.

Standards: The Rough Road to the Common Byte
(Libicki, 1995)

The inability of computers to "talk" to one another is a major problem, especially for today's high technology military forces. This study by the Center for Advanced Command Concepts and Technology looks at the growing but confusing body of information technology standards. Among other problems, it discovers a persistent divergence between the perspectives of the commercial user and those of the government.

What Is Information Warfare?*
(Libicki, 1995)

Is Information Warfare a nascent, perhaps embryonic art, or simply the newest version of a time-honored feature of warfare? Is it a new form of conflict that owes its existence to the burgeoning global information infrastructure, or an old one whose origin lies in the wetware of the human brain but has been given new life by the Information Age? Is it a unified field or opportunistic assemblage?

Operations Other Than War*
(Alberts & Hayes, 1995)

This report documents the fourth in a series of workshops and roundtables organized by the INSS Center for Advanced Concepts and Technology (ACT). The workshop sought insights into the process of determining what technologies are required for OOTW. The group also examined the complexities of introducing relevant technologies and discussed general and specific OOTW technologies and devices.

Dominant Battlespace Knowledge*
(Johnson & Libicki, 1996)

The papers collected here address the most critical aspects of that problem—to wit: If the United States develops the means to acquire dominant battlespace knowledge, how might that affect the way it goes to war, the circumstances under which force can and will be used, the purposes for its employment, and the resulting alterations of the global geomilitary environment?

Interagency and Political-Military Dimensions of Peace Operations: Haiti - A Case Study
(Hayes & Wheatley, 1996)

This report documents the fifth in a series of workshops and roundtables organized by the INSS Center for Advanced Concepts and Technology (ACT). Widely regarded as an operation that "went right," Haiti offered an opportunity to explore interagency relations in an operation close to home that had high visibility and a greater degree of interagency civilian-military coordination and planning than the other operations examined to date.

The Unintended Consequences of the Information Age*
(Alberts, 1996)

The purpose of this analysis is to identify a strategy for introducing and using Information Age technologies that accomplishes two things: first, the identification and avoidance of adverse unintended consequences associated with the introduction and utilization of information technologies; and second, the ability to recognize and capitalize on unexpected opportunities.

Joint Training for Information Managers*
(Maxwell, 1996)

This book proposes new ideas about joint training for information managers over Command, Control, Communications, Computers, and Intelligence (C4I) tactical and strategic levels. It suggests a substantially new way to approach the training of future communicators, grounding its argument in the realities of the fast-moving C4I technology.

Defensive Information Warfare*
(Alberts, 1996)

This overview of defensive information warfare is the result of an effort, undertaken at the request of the Deputy Secretary of Defense, to provide background material to participants in a series of interagency meetings to explore the nature of the problem and to identify areas of potential collaboration.

Command, Control, and the Common Defense
(Allard, 1996)

The author provides an unparalleled basis for assessing where we are and were we must go if we are to solve the joint and combined command and control challenges facing the U.S. military as it transitions into the 21st century.

Shock & Awe:
Achieving Rapid Dominance*
(Ullman & Wade, 1996)

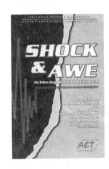

The purpose of this book is to explore alternative concepts for structuring mission capability packages around which future U. S. military forces might be configured.

Information Age Anthology:
Volume I*
(Alberts & Papp, 1997)

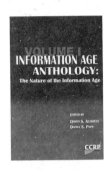

In this first volume, we will examine some of the broader issues of the Information Age: what the Information Age is; how it affects commerce, business, and service; what it means for the government and the military; and how it affects international actors and the international system.

Complexity, Global Politics,
and National Security*
(Alberts & Czerwinski, 1997)

The charge given by the President of the National Defense University and RAND leadership was three-fold: (1) push the envelope; (2) emphasize the policy and strategic dimensions of national defense with the implications for complexity theory; and (3) get the best talent available in academe.

Target Bosnia: Integrating Information Activities in Peace Operations*
(Siegel, 1998)

This book examines the place of PI and PSYOP in peace operations through the prism of NATO operations in Bosnia-Herzegovina.

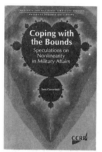

Coping with the Bounds
(Czerwinski, 1998)

The theme of this work is that conventional, or linear, analysis alone is not sufficient to cope with today's and tomorrow's problems, just as it was not capable of solving yesterday's. Its aim is to convince us to augment our efforts with nonlinear insights, and its hope is to provide a basic understanding of what that involves.

Information Warfare and International Law*
(Greenberg, Goodman, & Soo Hoo, 1998)

The authors, members of the Project on Information Technology and International Security at Stanford University's Center for International Security and Arms Control, have surfaced and explored some profound issues that will shape the legal context within which information warfare may be waged and national information power exerted in the coming years.

Lessons From Bosnia:
The IFOR Experience*
(Wentz, 1998)

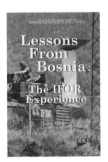

This book tells the story of the challenges faced and innovative actions taken by NATO and U.S. personnel to ensure that IFOR and Operation Joint Endeavor were military successes. A coherent C4ISR lessons learned story has been pieced together from firsthand experiences, interviews of key personnel, focused research, and analysis of lessons learned reports provided to the National Defense University team.

Doing Windows: Non-Traditional
Military Responses to Complex
Emergencies
(Hayes & Sands, 1999)

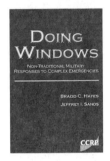

This book provides the final results of a project sponsored by the Joint Warfare Analysis Center. Our primary objective in this project was to examine how military operations can support the long-term objective of achieving civil stability and durable peace in states embroiled in complex emergencies.

Network Centric Warfare
(Alberts, Garstka, & Stein, 1999)

It is hoped that this book will contribute to the preparations for NCW in two ways. First, by articulating the nature of the characteristics of Network Centric Warfare. Second, by suggesting a process for developing mission capability packages designed to transform NCW concepts into operational capabilities.

Behind the Wizard's Curtain
(Krygiel, 1999)

There is still much to do and more to learn and under-stand about developing and fielding an effective and durable infostructure as a foundation for the 21st century. Without successfully fielding systems of systems, we will not be able to implement emerging concepts in adaptive and agile command and control, nor will we reap the potential benefits of Network Centric Warfare.

Confrontation Analysis: How to Win Operations Other Than War
(Howard, 1999)

A peace operations campaign (or operation other than war) should be seen as a linked sequence of confronta-tions, in contrast to a traditional, warfighting campaign, which is a linked sequence of battles. The objective in each confrontation is to bring about certain "compli-ant" behavior on the part of other parties, until in the end the campaign objective is reached. This is a state of sufficient compliance to enable the military to leave the theater.

Information Campaigns for Peace Operations
(Avruch, Narel, & Siegel, 2000)

In its broadest sense, this report asks whether the notion of struggles for control over information identifiable in situations of conflict also has relevance for situations of third-party conflict management—for peace operations.

Information Age Anthology: Volume II*
(Alberts & Papp, 2000)

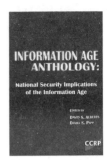

Is the Information Age bringing with it new challenges and threats, and if so, what are they? What sorts of dangers will these challenges and threats present? From where will they (and do they) come? Is information warfare a reality? This publication, Volume II of the Information Age Anthology, explores these questions and provides preliminary answers to some of them.

Information Age Anthology: Volume III*
(Alberts & Papp, 2001)

In what ways will wars and the military that fight them be different in the Information Age than in earlier ages? What will this mean for the U.S. military? In this third volume of the Information Age Anthology, we turn finally to the task of exploring answers to these simply stated, but vexing questions that provided the impetus for the first two volumes of the Information Age Anthology.

Understanding Information Age Warfare
(Alberts, Garstka, Hayes, & Signori, 2001)

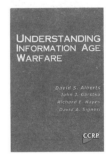

This book presents an alternative to the deterministic and linear strategies of the planning modernization that are now an artifact of the Industrial Age. The approach being advocated here begins with the premise that adaptation to the Information Age centers around the ability of an organization or an individual to utilize information.

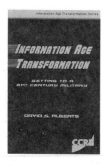

Information Age Transformation
(Alberts, 2002)

This book is the first in a new series of CCRP books that will focus on the Information Age transformation of the Department of Defense. Accordingly, it deals with the issues associated with a very large governmental institution, a set of formidable impediments, both internal and external, and the nature of the changes being brought about by Information Age concepts and technologies.

Code of Best Practice for Experimentation
(CCRP, 2002)

Experimentation is the lynch pin in the DoD's strategy for transformation. Without a properly focused, well-balanced, rigorously designed, and expertly conducted program of experimentation, the DoD will not be able to take full advantage of the opportunities that Information Age concepts and technologies offer.

Lessons From Kosovo: The KFOR Experience
(Wentz, 2002)

Kosovo offered another unique opportunity for CCRP to conduct additional coalition C4ISR-focused research in the areas of coalition command and control, civil-military cooperation, information assurance, C4ISR interoperability, and information operations.

NATO Code of Best Practice for C2 Assessment
(2002)

To the extent that they can be achieved, significantly reduced levels of fog and friction offer an opportunity for the military to develop new concepts of operations, new organisational forms, and new approaches to command and control, as well as to the processes that support it. Analysts will be increasingly called upon to work in this new conceptual dimension in order to examine the impact of new information-related capabilities coupled with new ways of organising and operating.

Effects Based Operations
(Smith, 2003)

This third book of the Information Age Transformation Series speaks directly to what we are trying to accomplish on the "fields of battle" and argues for changes in the way we decide what effects we want to achieve and what means we will use to achieve them.

The Big Issue
(Potts, 2003)

This Occasional considers command and combat in the Information Age. It is an issue that takes us into the realms of the unknown. Defence thinkers everywhere are searching forward for the science and alchemy that will deliver operational success.

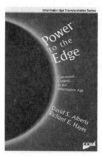

Power to the Edge:
Command...Control... in the
Information Age
(Alberts & Hayes, 2003)

Power to the Edge articulates the principles being used to provide the ubiquitous, secure, wideband network that people will trust and use, populate with high quality information, and use to develop shared awareness, collaborate effectively, and synchronize their actions.

Complexity Theory
and Network Centric Warfare
(Moffat, 2003)

Professor Moffat articulates the mathematical models and equations that clearly demonstrate the relationship between warfare and the emergent behaviour of complex natural systems, as well as a means to calculate and assess the likely outcomes.

Campaigns of Experimentation:
Pathways to Innovation and Transformation
(Alberts & Hayes, 2005)

In this follow-on to the Code of Best Practice for Experimentation, the concept of a campaign of experimentation is explored in detail. Key issues of discussion include planning, execution, achieving synergy, and avoiding common errors and pitfalls.

Somalia Operations: Lessons Learned (Allard, 2005)

Originally published by NDU in 1995, this book is Colonel Allard's examination of the challenges and the successes of the U.S. peacekeeping mission to Somalia in 1992-1994. Key topics include planning, deployment, conduct of operations, and support.